Slipping Through the Cracks

Slipping Through the Cracks

Intervention Strategies for Clients with Multiple Addictions and Disorders

Mark Sanders, LCSW, CADC

Health Communications, Inc.
Deerfield Beach, Florida

www.hcibooks.com

Library of Congress Cataloging-in-Publication Data

Sanders, Mark, 1960-
    Slipping through the cracks : intervention strategies for clients with multiple
addictions and disorders / Mark Sanders.
       p. cm.
    Includes bibliographical references and index.
    ISBN-13: 978-0-7573-1572-5 (trade paper)
    ISBN-10: 0-7573-1572-0 (trade paper)
    ISBN-13: 978-0-7573-9180-4 (e-book)
    ISBN-10: 0-7573-9180-X (e-book)
    1. Psychiatric social work.   2. Evidence based social work.   3. Social case
work.   4. Addicts--Counseling of.   5. Mentally ill--Counseling of.   I. Title.
HV689.S26 2011
362.2'0425--dc23

                                               2011031072

Publisher: Health Communications, Inc.
           3201 S.W. 15th Street
           Deerfield Beach, FL 33442–8190

Cover image ©iStockPhoto
Cover design by Larissa Hise Henoch
Interior design and formatting by Lawna Patterson Oldfield

Contents

To my friend and mentor William White.

Your example of hard work, statesmanship,

and writing genius is inspiring.

Acknowledgments

Special thanks to . . .

Peter Vegso, for agreeing to publish this manuscript.

Jeffrey Shore, for being the first to hire me as a
university instructor.

Tamara Shaffer, for typing this manuscript.

Stephanie Muller, for publishing many of my articles
in *Counselor* magazine.

Candace Johnson, for improving the quality of the
manuscript.

Introduction

THE SHIFT TOWARD evidence-based practices in addictions and behavioral health care is long overdue. For too long, practitioners in the behavioral health field have been led by what they believe will work rather than by evidence-based practices. This nonempirical approach has taken many forms, including counselors using "one-size-fits-all" models; using only the approach that worked during a brief stint in counseling; using only the therapeutic approach he or she "married" while in graduate school (leading to a difficult and painful "divorce"); using untested counseling techniques (turning clients into human guinea pigs); and, in some instances, being guided by "folklore" (beliefs and approaches that are passed on between generations of counselors through oral traditions without evidence of effectiveness). Today, the federal government is requiring applicants for grants to identify the evidence-based practices they plan to use. As federal funding sources demand the shift toward evidence-based practices, research suggests that this empirical approach will go a long way toward keeping more clients from slipping through the cracks (Miller 2009; Liddle and Rowe 2005; Emmelkamp and Vedel 2006).

In the midst of the movement toward evidence-based practices, there are many current realities that make the shift difficult and often cause a great deal of frustration. Many clients then continue to be at risk for relapse because their needs go unaddressed. Consider these current realities:

- Most evidence-based practices utilize individual and family therapy approaches, while practitioners in publicly funded addictions programs disproportionately utilize group interventions (Miller 2009). There has been a realization for quite some time by practitioners in the behavioral health field that group therapy is time effective and cost effective. If you meet with eight clients individually, it takes eight hours, but if you meet with them in a group, you can see all eight clients in one hour. While this is expedient, most of the evidence-based practices use individual and family approaches, not group therapy. This disparity tends, therefore, to disproportionally affect clients who are in publicly funded programs, and may create the opportunity for those clients to slip through the cracks.

- Effective implementation of an evidence-based practice requires fidelity to the model. In the era of budget cuts, many agencies cannot afford to hire a research team to ensure such fidelity. Minus such studies, there is no proof that the evidence-based practice is being utilized. Direct observation and feedback from clinical supervisors is necessary to ensure fidelity to an evidence-based practice (Miller 2009; SAMHSA TIP 52 2009). Without direct observation and feedback, supervisors in the addictions field have no clue what counselors are actually doing with clients.

- Premature termination of counseling. The longer clients are in treatment, the more progress they make, but approximately 50 percent of behavioral healthcare clients fail to make their second session (Duncan, Miller, and Sparks 2004). There are myriad causes of premature termination from therapy, including a mismatch between the counselor's approach and the client's needs or a mismatch between counseling priorities. When we are unable to engage clients, it is difficult to help them change.

- Counselors' natural resistance to change is inevitable when counselors have been practicing their approach to therapy for many years. They are so familiar with an approach that they can do it blindfolded. A change imposed from the outside will leave many counselors feeling uncomfortable, anxious, suddenly unsure of their skill set, and, in some instances, angry.

- Many clients have multiple problems and do not fit neatly

into the rubrics of an evidence-based practice. Numerous studies that prove the validity of an evidence-based practice are based upon clients who have a single problem or single diagnosis (Duncan, Miller, and Sparks 2004). Without a skill set specifically designed for these clients, counselors often rely on a hit-or-miss counseling approach, and clients may be treated for only one of their myriad problems, which may negate otherwise effective therapy.

The shift toward evidence-based practices in addiction and behavioral health care is especially challenging when counseling difficult-to-reach clients who have co-occurring disorders. At a recent seminar, one participant stated, "My clients are all HIV positive, chemically dependent, and have mental illness. There has never been an evidence-based approach developed with my clients in mind." In a focus group I facilitated on implementing evidence-based practices, a case manager stated, "My clients don't hit bottom; they live on the bottom. They lack the hope to stay around long enough to reap the benefits of an evidence-based practice." A school social worker stated, "I have a client who is a cutter with bulimia who drinks alcohol for breakfast. She lives in a constant state of crisis. I haven't seen one approach that fits her needs." A social worker from the Veterans Health Administration (VA) hospitals stated, "I work with returning Iraqi war veterans who suffer from post-traumatic stress disorder (PTSD) and addiction. Do you know how few, if any, evidence-based practices have been designed for this population?"

This book is written with such clients in mind—specifically, clients who have multiple problems that are rarely addressed in addictions, mental health, child welfare, or criminal justice settings. The goal of this book is to give counselors tools they can use to address the needs of difficult-to-reach clients who have multiple problems for which they seek therapy.

The specific client populations discussed in this book were selected from focus groups I facilitated with addictions counselors on clients they found most difficult to engage in counseling. Their list included clients who:

- are court mandated to counseling (Chapters 3, 8)
- have been diagnosed with antisocial personality disorder (Chapter 3)
- suffer from post-traumatic stress disorder (Chapter 4)
- suffer unresolved grief (Chapter 5)
- are addicted to highly addictive drugs such as cocaine, heroin, and methamphetamines (Chapter 3, 4, 6)
- are adolescents, who often don't believe they have a problem (Chapter 7)
- are lacking a motivation to change (Chapter 8)
- are from diverse backgrounds (Chapter 9)
- are chronic relapsers (Chapter 10)

In each chapter of this book, we will look at these populations and discuss their unique challenges. We also suggest intervention strategies for use in counseling them. Recovery management, an emerging model that has proven to be effective with difficult-to-reach, chemically dependent clients, is also discussed in detail. Finally, the book provides information on two evidence-based approaches that are effective in engaging multiproblem, difficult-to-reach clients in addictions treatment—motivational interviewing and the use of motivational incentives.

Counselors continue to note that they rarely see clients who have just a single problem. Their clients have more complex problems and are increasingly difficult to treat with each succeeding decade. While the movement toward evidence-based practices is a good idea (in that it requires us to provide more science in our work with clients), these approaches, with their definite techniques, offer the promise of driving on a smoothly paved highway. Many counselors report, however, that in the real world, there are often many bumps in the road. Difficult-to-reach clients do not always fit neatly into the rubrics of one evidence-based practice. This book is written to address those bumps in the road and to give counselors tools to help them work more effectively with difficult-to-reach clients who have multiple addictions and disorders.

one

Strategies for Engaging Resistant Clients

I T MAY SEEM OBVIOUS, but it is important to remember that an evidence-based practice cannot be implemented unless the client is engaged in treatment first. In the real world, only a small percentage of chemically dependent clients have a single problem (Hubble et al. 1999). Most show up at their first session with a combination of issues and often feel defensive and resistant to change. According to O'Connell and Beyer (2002), many chemically dependent clients are difficult to engage in counseling for myriad reasons, which include, but are not limited to:

- **Mandated status.** In the mid-1980s, the stigma of addiction increased due to the nation's response to the crack-cocaine epidemic and the war on drugs, and this led to more chemically dependent clients being mandated to treatment through the criminal justice and child welfare systems. In the more recent past, a disproportionately large number of clients receiving addictions treatment are either on probation, parole, awaiting trial, or incarcerated. Few people want to be told that they must go to counseling. This mandate automatically sets up resistance.

- **A lack of motivation to discontinue drug use.** The great majority of chemically dependent clients who enter treatment are ambivalent about whether or not they want to discontinue drug use. Some enter treatment only to take a short vacation from regular use. With programmatic goals that promote abstinence, resistance is automatically created among clients who are not motivated to stop using.

- **Discomfort opening up to strangers.** From the perspective of many clients, the counseling relationship is strange. The counselor knows everything about you, but you know next to nothing about him or her. In addition, drug use numbs emotions, and therapy tends to promote the expression of emotions, which can automatically create discomfort for clients. Both of these circumstances lead to resistance and make it difficult to engage chemically dependent clients in counseling.

- **Co-occurring conditions.** A combination of chemical
  dependence, mental illness, medical complications, brain
  damage, and other physical and mental conditions can
  make it difficult for clients to engage in traditional
  counseling. Clients can also be so focused on ailments
  that they lack hope that things can get better.

- **Multiple diagnoses.** With each diagnosis, there is the
  potential for denial, ambivalence, and resistance. The
  client may want to address some disorders and not others,
  while the counselor may think it important to address all
  disorders, which can automatically produce resistance. In
  addition, many counselors are not trained to recognize or
  treat every condition with which a client may present, so
  even without client resistance, there is the potential for
  client frustration and subsequent termination of counseling.

- **Difficult symptomatology.** There are myriad symptoms
  that accompany chemically dependent clients in
  treatment, including anger, rage, hostility, flat affect,
  depression, apathy, and feelings of hopelessness. If clients
  have co-occurring disorders, other complicating symptoms
  may include paranoia, delusional thinking, and hallucinations.
  If clients' brains have been damaged by drug use,
  symptoms might include short-term memory problems,
  confabulation, and difficulty with organizing thoughts
  and grasping materials discussed in counseling.

- **Initial therapeutic approaches that increase resistance.**
  There are a number of therapeutic approaches that have
  been found to increase client resistance, including
  confrontation techniques that leave chemically dependent
  clients feeling defensive; a lack of empathy, warmth, and
  genuineness; the therapist being the expert on the client's
  life rather than the client; and approaches that focus
  primarily on what the client is doing wrong rather than
  what the client is capable of doing right.

- **Unresolved grief.** Painful emotions connected to loss
  are difficult for clients to discuss and difficult for many
  helping professionals to broach. Handled poorly,
  addressing issues of grief can lead to premature
  termination (Sanders 2002a).

- **Unresolved trauma.** Many clients exposed to trauma
  suffer from symptoms of post-traumatic stress disorder,
  which can include flashbacks, nightmares, and frighten-
  ing thoughts and memories connected to the traumatic
  experiences. As in unresolved grief, discussing traumatic
  experiences can lead to resistance to counseling for myriad
  reasons, including the fact that clients may experience
  anxiety, terror, and post-traumatic symptoms as they
  discuss these issues in counseling.

- **Cross-cultural tension.** All counseling is cross-cultural
  because of issues of race, gender, religion, sexual
  orientation, age, and so forth (Sue and Sue 1990). Just

as tension can exist in the outside world related to cultural differences, it can also exist in counseling and serve as a barrier to establishing a satisfactory relationship between the counselor and the client.

- **Adolescence.** Adolescents often defy adult authority. With an increasing percentage of adolescents mandated to counseling, the counselor is automatically placed in a position of authority, which can evoke client resistance (Higgins et al. 2008). In addition, the great majority of adolescents with substance use disorders do not believe that they have a problem; they often lack motivation for long-term abstinence, and many of those who want to quit using would rather do so on their own than go to counseling (Higgins et al. 2008).

- **Negative prior counseling experiences.** Clients who have previously been in counseling bring preconceived notions about negative treatment experiences with them to subsequent treatment. These negative experiences include the use of heavy confrontation techniques, which leave clients feeling defensive. In the case of chemically dependent women, the majority of whom have been exposed to trauma, confrontation techniques have been found to retraumatize them (Straussner and Brown 2002). In cases where clients have relapsed while in previous treatment for chemical dependence and been discharged for that relapse, they are really proving that they are chemically dependent; thus, the program is discharging them for proving their diagnosis. This would never happen with a cancer patient, who would never be discharged for proving they have cancer.

• Negative experiences also include hostility expressed by group members that leaves clients feeling unsafe; low dosages of medication used during detoxification, which leaves clients experiencing heavy withdrawal during detox; family therapy utilized to give family members the opportunity to chastise the client for "destroying our lives" rather than to help the family heal; and aftercare as an after-thought: historically, the great majority of chemically dependent clients have been left on their own following discharge from treatment. It is no wonder, then, that 50 percent of chemically dependent clients fail to make their second counseling session (Miller and Rollnick 2002; White 2005).

Strategies for Engagement

There are numerous strategies counselors can use to engage clients successfully. The following have proven to be effective in reducing client resistance. They are also easy to implement regardless of the client's diagnosis or size of the therapeutic staff.

Exude Warmth, Beginning with Initial Contact

Research indicates that the warmth of a counselor's tone of voice communicated over the telephone prior to the first counseling session can decrease client dropout rates (Miller and Rollnick 2002). A warm greeting upon arrival at the agency at the first session can further reduce resistance, sending the message to clients that they are welcome.

Provide a Welcoming Atmosphere

When clients are met with a friendly greeting from a receptionist and are invited into a waiting room that contains plants, pictures on the wall, pleasant music, and other niceties, they feel welcomed and valued, and this can go a long way to facilitating rapport. Minkoff and Cline (2004) have described the creation of a welcoming environment for clients as a necessary and promising practice. Many clients have experienced stigma in the larger community and begin counseling feeling as though they have failed. Many other clients enter counseling feeling "less than." Providing a welcoming environment can be humanizing and equalizing. Noted psychiatrist Kenneth Minkoff travels the country giving workshops to receptionists on how to welcome clients into their agencies. It sends the message to clients that "you are welcome and we see you as valuable." This can automatically reduce client resistance.

Offer a Snack While the Client Waits

Extending this hospitality either within the first few minutes of contact or as the client leaves each session can be instrumental in reducing client resistance. Research by Petry and Bohn (2003) reveals that the use of low-cost incentives such as candy bars, vouchers, small cash awards, and clinic privileges have been effective in increasing engagement, attendance, and programmatic retention and decreasing resistance in addictions treatment.

Focus on Clients' Strengths

Many chemically dependent clients are defensive and resistant to counseling because they feel they have failed. A strength-based approach can decrease that defensiveness (Sharry 2004). Counseling approaches that focus too much on what clients have done wrong, rather than on what they are capable of doing right, leave clients feeling defensive and resistant to counseling (Duncan 2005). Clients are often asked questions in the initial intake session that increase their feelings of stigmatization and defensiveness, such as:

- How much do you drink?
- How many times have you relapsed?
- Have you ever been treated for mental illness?
- How many times were you hospitalized?
- Have you ever attempted suicide? How many times?
- Have you ever had a venereal disease?
- Have you ever shared a dirty needle?
- Have you ever been arrested? How many times? How many felonies?

Strength-based questions can be instrumental in decreasing client resistance and facilitating engagement (Sharry 2004). Examples include:

- What do you do well?
- How have you been able to endure so much?
- What do you like to do in your leisure time?
- What are the best three moments you can recall in your life?
- What is the best thing you have ever made happen?
- What is your previous life suffering preparing you to do with the rest of your life?
- Which of your life challenges have taught you the most about your own resilience?
- What sources of strength did you draw from as you faced these challenges?
- What have you learned from what you've gone through?

Explore the Client's Past Experience with Counseling

The longer the treatment career of chemically dependent clients, the greater the probability that they have had negative treatment experiences that can impact your ability to engage them in counseling. Eighty percent of relapses occur within the first ninety days of clients leaving treatment (GLATTC Bulletin 2005). Fewer than 30 percent of chemically dependent clients receive ninety days of support following discharge; thus, they have not received the support needed to remain sober (White, Kurtz, and Sanders 2006). If the client's previous experience was negative, let him or her know how the experience will be different with you.

Ask the following questions to gauge the client's previous experience in counseling:

1. Have you worked with an addictions counselor in the past?
2. What was that experience like for you?
3. What worked? What did not work?
4. What aspect of your previous counseling experience was most helpful for you? What was least helpful?
5. In working with you as your counselor, what are some things that I should never do?

Again, if the client mentions things that did not work in previous counseling or were harmful, take the time to outline how your approach will be different. For instance:

Client: "My counselor tried to force me to attend AA meetings, and I was not interested in attending them; they talk so much about God there. When we would go to groups, clients would often yell and scream at each other, leaving us feeling frightened. It reminded me of when I lived with my parents: my father would come home drunk and yell and scream at us. This made me want to leave treatment."

Counselor: "We know so much more now about recovery than we did in the past, and one of the things that we've learned is the benefit of sharing options other than Alcoholics Anonymous to help people recover. Two things I will do differently are talk to you about the type of recovery support you prefer and share with you a list of alternatives to Alcoholics Anonymous. I also believe that safety in group counseling is very important, so I work hard as a group leader to help keep things safe. I believe it is an important part of recovery to express your feelings. I try to help group members express themselves in a safe manner, so if you're ever feeling unsafe or if things feel out of control, you can let us know."

Utilize Stage-Based Interventions

Research reveals that stage-based interventions are effective in facilitating rapport with clients (SAMHSA 2008; Rosengren 2009). Many chemically dependent clients are in various stages of readiness to change (DiClemente 2007). Stage-based interventions can be particularly effective with clients who have multiple problems because they allow the counselor to base intervention strategies on the client's level of readiness to change each problem (DiClemente 2007). These stages include:

- **Precontemplation.** The client is unaware of having a problem or needing to make a change, and is therefore not considering the possibility of change.
- **Contemplation.** The client is aware of the problem but is ambivalent about making a change.

- **Determination.** The client is motivated to do something about the problem but has not yet taken the initiative to make a change.

- **Action.** The client engages in action for the purpose of bringing about change.

- **Maintenance.** The client engages in behavior to sustain the change. When a chemically dependent client is in the maintenance stage, abstinence has been observed for six months or longer (DiClemente 2007).

Consider the client who has schizophrenia and alcoholism. As it pertains to addressing alcoholism, this client is in the action stage, evidenced by the fact that the client attends daily AA meetings, has weekly contact with a 12-step sponsor, and participates in sober activities at the local Alanon fellowship. But the client also refuses to take medication, see a psychiatrist, or have contact with a case manager concerning mental illness. This client is clearly in the precontemplation stage as it pertains to mental illness.

Minimize Confrontation

At the Ohio Statewide Addictions Conference in 2006, a noted speaker stated, "There is no such thing as a resistant client, only helpers who struggle to accept clients where they are in their recovery."

Confrontation leads to resistance and premature termination. There are studies that report a strong link between counselor confrontation and clients returning to drug use. In one study comparing cognitive behavioral group therapy with confrontational group therapy, the dropout rate was four times higher in the confrontational group. In another study comparing behavior modification with confrontational therapy, the improvement rate was fifty times higher in the group receiving behavior modification. Another study revealed that chemically dependent clients with low self-esteem are harmed by confrontation, and their recidivism rates are higher because of this confrontation. In a study comparing confrontation versus the client-centered approach to counseling, those receiving the client-centered approach showed a larger reduction in alcohol use than those receiving the confrontational approach (White and Miller 2007).

Engage in Mutual Treatment Planning

This egalitarian, respectful approach allows the client to be a partner in his or her own counseling (Corey 2000), and allows the client to have an equal voice in his or her care. Research reveals that people are more likely to make positive change if they choose the pathway (Rosengren 2009). Mutual treatment planning also respects the client's right to self-determination and automatically reduces resistance (Miller and Rollnick 2002).

Far too often, counselors complete treatment plans for clients and wonder why they encounter resistance. Mutual treatment planning can begin with the counselor asking the client a variety of questions, such as:

- What would you like to see different in your life?
- What would you like to change?
- What would you like to accomplish in therapy?
- What outcome would you like counseling to achieve?
- If you had a magic wand, and by waving it, your life would suddenly be different, what would be different in your life?
- What, if anything, would you like to accomplish in the next thirty days?

Avoid Power Struggles

Power struggles decrease engagement and can lead to premature termination (Rosengren 2009). This is particularly true for clients who are mandated and/or resistant to counseling (Miller and Rollnick 1990). There are a number of measures you can take to avoid power struggles:

- **Remind yourself of the client's right to self-determination.** Clients have the right to make their own choices in life—including bad choices—and a counselor needs to remember this important principle. Imposing your will on the client can lead to power struggles.

- **View a power struggle as a sign that you need to either slow down or change direction**. When your comments or interventions are met with resistance, simply acknowledging the resistance can keep the alliance positive.

- **Comment on the client's body language**. For example, when the client looks uncomfortable with a suggestion to attend a 12-step program, a counselor has the opportunity to suggest other pathways to recovery.

Avoid Early Labels

The term "early labels" refers to giving clients premature diagnoses such as cocaine dependent, antisocial personality disorder, schizophrenic, and so forth, prior to establishing rapport. Early labels can lead to clients feeling defensive and being more difficult to engage (Rosengren 2009). Relationship building should precede early labels/diagnoses; it is easier to receive feedback from someone you trust and with whom you have a relationship.

Early labeling can lead to clients spending years trying to prove their counselors wrong. In the case of mental illness, this might be done by avoiding taking psychiatric medication and receiving mental health treatment; in the case of addiction, clients can spend years trying to prove their counselors wrong by avoiding addictions treatment, 12-step participation, and trying to teach themselves controlled drinking or drug use. Because chemical dependence and mental illness carry stigmas in our society, many clients meet the initial diagnoses with a decrease in self-esteem and may flee therapy to avoid the resultant feelings.

Be Willing to Have a Sensitive Discussion About Race, Gender, and Other Differences

Differences in viewpoints between counselor and client in race, gender, socioeconomic standing, religion, age, worldview, and other subjects can be a barrier to successful counseling. A good time to have a discussion of differences is when you sense that these differences are barriers to effective communication and rapport building (Sue and Sue 2007).

Ask for Permission to Give Feedback

For many years, addictions counselors have given clients unsolicited feedback in a confrontational style (White and Miller 2007), which leaves many clients feeling uncomfortable. When feedback is filled with opinions that are presented in a confrontational way, therapeutic walls instead of therapeutic bridges are often created (SAMHSA 2008).

Be Aware of Countertransference Reactions

By definition, countertransference involves negative reactions that counselors have toward their clients (Corey 2000). Counselors who have negative reactions to their clients (which often increase those clients' resistance to counseling) can use those reactions to seek supervision, therapy, peer support, or education to work with them effectively. Many difficult-to-reach clients with substance use disorders have myriad behaviors that are easy to judge because they victimize others by their behaviors. These behaviors include (but are not limited to) DUI offenses, theft, antisocial behavior, physical abuse, sexual abuse, and domestic violence. Each person with a substance use disorder directly affects seven people (Kinney 2002). As counselors listen to the stories from clients and/or significant others who have been harmed by the clients' addictions, it is easy to have negative reactions to their clients.

Sigmund Freud indicated that countertransference was something to avoid completely (Corey 2000). Modern psychoanalysts view countertransference in a different light, however—as a gift that allows personal and professional growth for the counselor that can then add to the effectiveness of the counseling experience for the client.

I once provided supervision in a hospital setting to a new counselor who was learning motivational interviewing skills, a nonconfrontational approach in which the client leads and the counselor follows (Miller and Rollnick 2002). I noted that she used the model effectively with cancer patients, kidney dialysis patients, those in the emergency room, and practically all other types of patients—with the exception of diabetics. When she met with diabetic patients, she would deviate from the model and give those clients lectures on how they should take care of their health; that made the patients visibly uncomfortable. When I asked the counselor about this, her answer was, "My mother and father both died from diabetes, so when I meet with a diabetic, it becomes personal." This was an eye-opener for her, and she learned that she needed to do more work around the deaths of her parents to keep her personal experiences from negatively affecting her work with diabetics.

Honor a Variety of Approaches to Recovery

The addictions field has a history of assuming that there is only one way that people recover—treatment followed by 12-step program attendance. While this one-dimensional approach has helped many, it has produced a great deal of resistance in others. As the field of addictions treatment grows, we are learning that clients have success with a variety of approaches to recovery. These approaches include solo interactions, 12-step programs, religious styles, medication-assisted, harm reduction, virtual participation, and cultural pathways. Honoring the client's pathway to recovery can be instrumental in reducing resistance (White, Kurtz, and Sanders 2005).

Maintain a Sense of Humor

Comedian and pianist Victor Borge said, "Laughter is the shortest distance between two people." Humor in therapy can reduce resistance (Buckmin 1994). Famous poet and author Maya Angelou told Oprah Winfrey that only those who have equal standing laugh with each other. Many clients who have multiple problems carry a great deal of stigma that leaves them feeling *less than*, but laughter can be the great equalizer (Buckmin 1994).

In addition to being a great equalizer, humor can also humanize the counselor by demonstrating that the counselor is willing to have fun, lighten up, and not always be serious. (See "How to Use Humor in Counseling" below for suggestions about using humor.) Humor can also decrease cross-cultural tension and build trust in cross-cultural counseling (Buckmin 1994). It can allow some relief from both emotional and physical pain. It can also allow clients to change how they perceive a situation. It can ease anxiety and make therapeutic time seem to go by more quickly. Laughter can facilitate self-disclosure by creating a friendly environment.

HOW TO USE HUMOR IN COUNSELING

Engage in planned spontaneity. Many counselors agree that the best humor by counselors is thoughtfully spontaneous, well timed, and takes into consideration who the client is. The goal should be to lessen client tension, increase client comfort, and/or help the client gain insight.

Use exaggeration. Sometimes making a situation seem bigger than it is can help the client see the absurdity of his or her concern.

Client: "I missed a 12-step meeting yesterday to go to my mother's eightieth birthday party. I feel like I abandoned my recovery regimen."

Counselor: "Oh, wow! The world must be coming to an end."

Client laughs.

Counselor: "Actually, an important part of recovery is spending healthy time with relatives and celebrating special occasions."

Client: "You're right. When I was getting high, I never attended family functions."

Change dialects. When counselors change dialects, clients can often find the humor in a situation. Examples include using the voice of both an adult and an adolescent when talking to an adolescent, or alternating voices between an older and a younger person.

Take a "funny bone history." As a part of intake, it is helpful to find out the types of things that make the client laugh. Such an inquiry can help balance out resistance-producing questions such as "How much do you drink?" and "How much marijuana do you smoke?" Topics covered might include what types of humor the client enjoys, whether or not he or she enjoys telling or hearing jokes, and the types of humor others find amusing that do not appeal to the client. The answers will offer insight about the client's specific sense of humor.

Utilize reframes. This technique is based on the Eastern practice of *paradox*, the idea that two statements can be true about a subject at the same time. When used effectively, a reframe can reduce client resistance, instill hope, help him or her view a situation differently, and lead to laughter, which can automatically reduce tension in counseling (Sanders 2005). Reframes can also give clients a different way of looking at a situation. For example:

Adolescent client: "My father yells at me a lot."

Counselor: "It sounds like he really wants you to hear him."

Adolescent client: "He says I'm stubborn."

Counselor: "It sounds like you have a mind of your own."

Adolescent client: "Yes, I keep getting high in spite of the fact that I've had six treatments. I'm a failure."

Counselor: "Six treatments! It sounds like you're determined to get sober one day."

Adolescent client: "That's right. That's why I'm here."

Offer a menu of options. At a recent seminar, a participant who works with resistant and mandated adolescents told me her agency uses a large menu that resembles a restaurant menu, but it happens to be about four feet tall. The counseling services provided by the agency are written on this menu. She hands it to clients during the first session and allows them to pick the services they want. When clients see this large menu they often chuckle, and that is the beginning of rapport-building between counselor and client.

Make fun of yourself. Some counselors will poke fun at themselves, telling stories about mistakes they have made in the past. This can facilitate rapport with resistant clients; in addition to producing laughter, it also sends the message that the counselor is imperfect, which, of course, can give clients the message that they do not have to be perfect.

Use humor prompts. Some counselors have humor prompts in their offices, which also send the signal that the counselor can see the lighter side of things. These might include movie clips, cartoons, anecdotes, signs, or masks.

Point out absurdities and illogical reasoning. While clients sometimes have difficulty understanding the logic of an abstract or general statement, they often have a clearer understanding when they can relate the concept to their own situation. Here's an example:

> **Counselor:** "On the one hand you said you want to be the next LeBron James on the basketball court, and earlier you told me you smoke a pack of cigarettes and five marijuana joints a day. I'm visualizing you running down the basketball court with a cigarette in one hand and a joint in the other."
>
> **Client [laughing]:** "Yes, but if I really want to play professional basketball, I need stamina, and smoking takes away a lot of my energy."

The primary purpose of humor is to help the client; inappropriate humor can be hurtful to clients. Laughing *at* the client, taking cheap shots, using sarcasm, and telling racist and sexist jokes are all inappropriate in a counseling setting.

Abraham Maslow, the founder of humanistic psychology, said, "If your only tool is a hammer, you tend to see every problem as a nail." (http://www.quotegarden.com/perspective.html). Adding to your toolbox of techniques will increase the likelihood that you will be able to effectively engage difficult-to-reach clients with substance use disorders. We hope you find some of these strategies useful in your efforts to help difficult-to-reach clients in their recovery journey.

two

Integrating the Addictions and Mental Health Recovery Movements

IN THE 1930S AND 1940S, there was a strong working alliance between the recovery and mental health professions. Noteworthy was Bill W.'s correspondence with Carl Jung, the renowned psychiatrist, on the spiritual nature of alcoholism. Dr. William Silkworth, author of the foreword to the *Big Book of Alcoholics Anonymous*, noted that the alcoholic was sick in mind, spirit, body, and soul and that there needed to be a collaboration between the recovery and psychiatric communities (Blocker, Fahey, and Tyrrell 2003).

Over the course of the past seventy-five years, a rift has been created between the addictions and mental health fields. The biggest consequence of this rift has been numerous clients with co-occurring conditions slipping through the cracks (SAMHSA TIP 42 2005). The addictions field has contributed to this rift by:

- Ignoring clients' psychiatric symptoms.
- Ignoring the fact that many clients with co-occurring disorders need to take medication and instead chanting the simple mantra, "a drug is a drug is a drug."
- Discharging clients when they exhibit psychiatric symptoms without addressing possible mental illness issues.
- Refusing to uniformly and collectively increase knowledge of mental illness and mental health treatment.
- Stigmatizing clients for having mental illness.
- Triggering decomposition through the use of heavy confrontation (White and Miller 2007).

The mental health field has contributed to this rift by:

- Enabling addiction to progress by not identifying it and addressing it in treatment.
- Prescribing addictive medication to clients addicted to alcohol and/or elicit drugs (thereby facilitating addiction to prescription medication).
- Stigmatizing and discharging clients for being chemically dependent.

- Promoting therapeutic approaches that have failed to turn alcoholics into social drinkers and thus facilitating numerous relapses.
- Harboring biases against referring clients to 12-step groups.
- Diagnosing mental illness prematurely in clients with substance use disorders (SAMHSA TIP 42 2005).

The result of this rift between the two fields is that the needs of clients with co-occurring disorders often go unaddressed. Thus, they are part of the revolving door syndrome, traveling back and forth seeking services between each system without getting all of their needs met. As a result, clients with co-occurring disorders have more psychiatric hospitalizations, addiction treatment readmissions, arrests, evictions, suicide attempts, and actual suicides than clients with a single diagnosis of addiction or mental illness (Muesser et al. 2003).

Change is clearly needed.

And change is coming. But the addictions and mental health fields are simultaneously going through separate recovery revolutions without either side knowing much about the other's movements.

The Addictions Recovery Movements

There are two movements occurring in the addictions field—one is a recovery advocacy movement and the other is a recovery management treatment movement. They were triggered in the 1980s and 1990s by the criminalization of addiction. During those years, the crack-cocaine epidemic prompted insurance companies to use that criminalization to decrease their coverage of substance use disorders, leaving only outpatient treatment as a primary option for clients whose illnesses may have been chronic.

The **recovery advocacy movement** is being led by individuals in recovery, their families, and visionary professionals in the addictions field (White, Kurtz, and Sanders 2005). These groups are advocating for:

- Long-term recovery.
- Greater emphasis placed on recovery rather than on treatment.
- An end to discrimination by insurance companies who routinely pay less for addictions treatment than they do for other medical conditions.
- A recognition of multiple pathways to long-term recovery.
- Individuals in recovery having a voice in the direction of that recovery.
- Treatment as an alternative to incarceration.
- The restoration of citizenship. (See "Restoring Citizenship" on page 33 for more on this critical component of the recovery advocacy movement.)

RESTORING CITIZENSHIP

The restoration of "citizenship" is especially important for individuals in recovery. This common term—used in both the addictions and criminal justice fields—does not mean that individuals are no longer U.S. citizens. What it often means in many states is that once you receive a felony conviction, you lose the right to vote and to work various jobs—including at places like McDonald's and Walgreen's, among others. In some states, you also lose the right to receive grants for college. You are ineligible for public housing and food stamps, and if your crime was drug-related you could also lose the use of your driver's license. Therefore, even if you get a job you may not be allowed to drive to work. In many states, to work in some occupations you have to have a state license. In the state of Illinois, for example, there are eighty-one occupations that require licenses that individuals are ineligible for if they have a felony conviction. These include a license to practice clinical social work, barbering, and a license to trim hedges in peoples' yards. Illinois Congressman Danny K. Davis was able to get a bill passed successfully in Congress that allows ex-felons who have committed nonviolent crimes to have their records expunged if they complete various programs. In states where people are not allowed to vote because they have felonies, advocacy groups are fighting to have this right restored. There are clinical programs that are encouraging clients to vote, acquire Social Security cards, complete their GEDs, go to community college, complete job readiness programs, secure employment, volunteer in their communities, and participate in block parties as a way of "restoring their own citizenship"—that is, doing the things that people stop doing once they develop an active addiction.

The recovery management treatment movement is one that shifts away from treating addiction in short-term, acute episodes toward a long-term approach similar to the way other progressive and chronic illnesses such as cancer and diabetes are treated (White 2005). This movement involves:

- Placing a greater emphasis on long-term recovery rather than on treatment.
- Focusing on the importance of continuous care rather than treating aftercare "like an afterthought" (GLATTC Bulletin 2005).
- Acknowledging that clients are utilizing multiple paths to long-term recovery.
- Giving clients a voice in the direction of their treatment and recovery.
- Using indigenous healers (recovery coaches) who work with clients on an ongoing basis in clients' natural environments.
- Forming new partnerships among treatment, faith-based, secular, and other communities of recovery.

While these revolutions have been occurring in the addictions field, a similar paradigm shift is occurring in the mental health arena.

The Mental Health Recovery Movement

This movement has been triggered by a number of events, including the closing of many state hospitals nationwide, leaving consumers of mental health services to forge their own mental health recovery movement. The movement is led by consumers, family members, and professionals in the mental health field who are advocating for effective mental health treatment. They are working to end discrimination by insurance companies who routinely attempt, as they have in addiction cases, to cover this care at lower rates than for other medical conditions (SAMHSA 2004; www.nami.org). The tenets of this "person-centered movement" (SAMHSA 2004) include:

- The client has ownership of his or her life and is therefore the director of his or her plan.

- Clients have a greater investment in the change process if they choose their own path.

- Family and friends who believe in the client can be great sources of support.

- Services are geared toward helping the client achieve a desired future and a meaningful life.

- The client is approached as a capable human being who is full of strengths.

- What the client has learned from previous experiences should be included in the plan.

- Helpers work to view the situation from the client's perspective.

- Wellness strategies chosen by the client are used.

- Service planning should include the client's entire life.

- The helpers strive to understand the client's uniqueness, hopes, wishes, dreams, and aspirations.

Integrating the Recovery Movements

The commonalities between the addictions and mental health recovery movements lend themselves well to integration, and research reveals that an integrated approach to co-occurring disorders in treatment and recovery is the most effective (Muesser et al. 2003). In both recovery movements, integrated approaches are:

- Individualized.

- Rooted in the belief that there is no one pathway to recovery.

- Longitudinal in their perspective.

- Strength-based.

- Egalitarian.

- Centered in the client's natural environment.

- Respectful of diversity and utilize indigenous healers in recovery.

- Peer-based.

- Deeply rooted in the belief that clients and their families have the capacity to grow and change.

Each time we provide services for clients who would ordinarily slip through the cracks, we play a major role in strengthening recovery. Counselors can take several steps to accelerate this integration on an individual level. They include:

- Learning more about the other fields' recovery movements.
- Having a peer mentor from another discipline as a teacher/guide.
- Volunteering to do cross-training. An addictions counselor can volunteer to work at a mental health center, and vice versa.
- Allowing clients to teach about how they have slipped through the cracks in the past. Discover from them what worked, what did not work, and what the holes in the system were.
- Being a change agent within your organization. Change does not always have to start from the top: it can begin in the middle or at the bottom of the ladder. At a staff meeting, consider talking with staff members about the need to integrate the addictions and mental health recovery movements. You may suggest that your organization offer workshops for staff to learn more about this subject. You may volunteer to do a workshop yourself at your agency to share what you have learned about this subject.

If this integration is going to occur, policy makers and funding sources will have to be on board with the idea of funding integrated programs. Leaders from both fields will have to come together to discuss their philosophical differences, both at the micro and macro levels. There will need to be cross-training for addictions and mental health professionals, and counselors must make a concerted effort to attend staff meetings of the other organization. The client's voice will have to be a part of all discussions concerning his or her care, including at the policy level, and strategic plans will have to be created to help guard against each field's instincts to bounce back to the "old way of doing business." The necessary work will be worth the effort, however, as a way to ensure more clients benefit from the integration of treatments, and fewer clients slip through the cracks.

three

Antisocial Personality Disorder, Criminality, and Substance Use Disorders

S OME OF THE MOST DIFFICULT-TO-REACH CLIENTS are those who suffer from antisocial personality disorder, criminality, and addiction disorders (Rotgers and Maniacci 2006). These clients are at risk of becoming a part of the triple revolving-door syndrome, meaning they are more likely to be involved in drug use, street crime, and incarceration. The majority of clients diagnosed with antisocial personality disorder have a concurrent substance use disorder (Black 1999). They often have a pattern of going back and forth between street crime (the money from which is used to support their drug habit) and incarceration. The pattern can repeat itself for years.

Contributing to the problem is the fact that these clients often have feelings of entitlement, a lack of remorse, a lack of empathy for those they have victimized, or an inability to see their part in any dispute. They are often difficult to engage in counseling as they bring cognitive distortions to treatment. These clients also receive strong countertransference reactions from counselors because they prey on society. They are the clients of choice for few clinicians. Yet, untreated antisocial personality disorder is costly to society in terms of prison sentences, crime, and victimization. Keeping these clients from slipping through the cracks not only helps them and their immediate families but benefits society as a whole.

Common Characteristics of Clients with Antisocial Personality Disorder

The *Diagnostic and Statistical Manual of Mental Disorders, Vol. IV-TR* (DSM-IV-TR) outlines the criteria for antisocial personality disorder (American Psychiatric Association 2000). The criteria begin with noting that the individual is at least eighteen years old at the time of diagnosis, and has demonstrated a pervasive pattern of disregard for, and violation of, the rights of others occurring since age fifteen years of age as indicated by three or more of the following:

- Failure to conform to social norms with respect to lawful behaviors.

- Deceitfulness.

- Impulsivity or failure to plan ahead.

- Occurrence is not exclusively during the course of schizophrenia or a manic episode.

- Irritability and aggressiveness (repeated physical fights or assault).

- Reckless disregard for safety of others or self.

- Consistent irresponsibility.

- Lack of remorse.

Other common characteristics include:

Incarceration. Fifty percent of those with antisocial personality disorder have spent one or more years in prison (Black 1999). Many become institutionalized and function better in prison than in society.

Substance use disorders. More than 70 percent of individuals diagnosed with antisocial personality disorder have a concurrent substance use disorder (Black 1999). Those with co-occurring disorders have more arrests, more evictions, and more hospitalizations than those with a single diagnosis of mental illness or addiction (SAMHSA TIP 42 2005).

Aggression. Many people with antisocial personality disorder have histories of violence directed toward society as a whole. They can be quite intimidating to counselors, thus making it difficult to engage them in counseling. They often sit in therapy with a silent rage; this leaves the counselor feeling uncomfortable and sometimes unwilling to challenge the client out of fear.

Irresponsibility. Many clients with antisocial personality disorder have years of unemployment, underemployment, and spotty work histories. Many live off their parents' incomes and refuse to make child support payments.

Cognitive distortions. Cognitive distortions involve faulty, exaggerated, or irrational thinking. These distortions include:

Feelings of entitlement.

Lack of remorse (blaming others).

Polarized thinking; believing the world is either good or bad.

Justifying actions.

Personal infallibility.

Narcissism.

Lack of empathy.

Belief that other people are irrelevant.

(Rotgers and Maniacci 2006; Ekleberry 2009)

In Search of the Conscience

The lack of apparent remorse often displayed by these clients after they commit crimes can leave clinicians wondering, "Where is the conscience?" It is helpful for clinicians to understand the factors that contribute to the development of antisocial personality disorder so they can implement appropriate intervention strategies. These contributing factors include conduct disorder, male depression, abandonment, a killed spirit, genetics, bullying behavior, behavioral problems, and family dynamics. Let's look at these factors in more detail.

Conduct Disorder

A prerequisite to a diagnosis of antisocial personality disorder is the diagnosis of conduct disorder in childhood or adolescence. In fact, more than 40 percent of those diagnosed with conduct disorder by adolescence go on to develop antisocial personality disorder in adulthood (Black 1999). According to the *DSM-IV-TR*, the criteria for conduct disorder include a repetitive and persistent pattern of behavior in which the basic rights of others or major age-appropriate societal norms or rules are violated. There have also been recent displays of several of the following behaviors: aggression toward people and animals; destruction of property; deceitfulness or theft; serious violations of rules; *and* the disturbance in behavior causes clinically significant impairment in social, academic, or occupational functioning (American Psychiatric Association 2000).

Abandonment

Many of those diagnosed with antisocial personality disorder were abandoned as children by one or both parents (Black 1999).

It is common for those abandoned to express shame. Those who develop conduct disorder followed by antisocial personality disorder may display this shame by acting shameless (Garbarino 1999), which explains the apparent absence of remorse when they victimize society. The abandonment in early childhood is often medicated later with alcohol and other drugs.

A Killed Spirit

Eighty percent of adolescent males who murder have a diagnosis of conduct disorder (which, as mentioned earlier, is a prerequisite for receiving the diagnosis of antisocial personality disorder). Many appear to have a killed spirit, enabling them to depersonalize during the process of killing others. There are four circumstances that kill a human spirit (Garbarino 1999): lack of love, rejection, victimization in abuse (physical, emotional, sexual, verbal, and others), and constant instability (evictions, relocations, and related issues).

Male Depression

The root cause of male depression is the absence of a positive father-son relationship (Real 1997). Many men are robbed of a feeling vocabulary in childhood by adult caretakers. The message they receive is that men should keep their feelings to themselves. Minus a feeling vocabulary—permission and practice to share hurt—their later depression shows up disguised as anger or rage followed by violence. Another symptom of adolescent male depression is the early use of alcohol and other drugs to numb feelings connected to the absence of a father figure (Real 1997). This diagnosis is often missed in adolescent males, because anger and rage do not look like classic depression.

Genetics

Twenty percent of individuals diagnosed with antisocial personality disorder have a first-degree relative who also has a diagnosis of antisocial personality disorder (Black 1999).

Bullying Behavior

Individuals who bully others in elementary and middle school are likely to have experienced corporal punishment at home (Remboldt and Zimmerman 1998). They go to school and repeat what happens to them by victimizing other children. If children who bully others were charged as adults, the charges would include assault, battery, extortion, theft, and kidnapping. By high school, many of these individuals become marginalized; they are no longer the biggest and toughest kids in the school. They are often involved in drugs, often wind up dropping out of school, and are vulnerable to a life of crime and other antisocial behaviors (Remboldt and Zimmerman 1998).

Behavioral Problems

Adolescents who are difficult to control in school environments may end up with a special education placement; there, they are often surrounded by other youth who are angry and who use drugs. In such an environment, antisocial behavior can thrive as a learned behavior and coping mechanism.

Family Dynamics

Many individuals diagnosed with an antisocial personality disorder are from families where there is a great deal of turmoil, abandonment, abuse, and/or drug use (Black 1999). As with the other factors listed, there is a strong link between antisocial personality disorder and addiction.

Diagnosing Antisocial Personality Disorder

When a client has a persistent history of crime and incarceration, it is wise to consider antisocial personality disorder as a diagnosis, keeping in mind that while many individuals addicted to drugs such as cocaine, methamphetamines, and heroin often engage in antisocial behavior to support their addiction, they may not meet the *DSM-IV-TR* criteria for antisocial personality disorder, which includes evidence of conduct disorder prior to age fifteen.

When attempting to determine whether a client meets the criteria for this diagnosis, the counselor must make a sincere attempt to build rapport with the client during the data-gathering phase. Your job is to be a therapeutic change agent, not a prosecuting attorney. To this end, ask specific questions that can help confirm or rule out the diagnosis.

If the client is a child or adolescent, here are some appropriate questions:

- Do you get into frequent fights?
- Have you ever destroyed property?
- Have you ever been expelled from school?
- Have you ever hurt animals?
- Do you ever steal or break into homes?
- Do you ever set fires?
- Do you often violate curfew?
- Have you ever been placed in a detention center or alternative school?
- Have you ever run away from home?
- Do you feel as though the world "owes" you?

When the client is an adult, the questions should be more directed to that age group:

- Have you ever been arrested as an adult? If yes, how many times?
- Have you ever used weapons?
- Do you have any felonies?
- Have you ever had difficulty keeping a job? If yes, why?
- Have you ever quit a job out of anger?
- Do you ever think about seriously harming someone?
- Can you tell me about your alcohol and drug use?

- Have you ever tried to con others?
- Have you ever felt unconcerned after hurting others?
- Have there ever been times when you felt that the world owes you?

In determining whether or not the client has antisocial personality disorder, interviews with the client's relatives and friends can often be helpful. They can provide information about the client's conduct and behavior during his or her youth and adulthood. A little detective work can also pay off: hospital, educational, military, psychiatric treatment, and addictions treatment records can also be helpful in making a diagnosis. And finally, determine if the client was ever in a gang, hate group, or destructive peer group. Those diagnosed with antisocial personality disorder have histories of involvement with destructive peer groups (O'Connell and Beyer 2002).

The Treatment of Antisocial Personality Disorder and Addiction

One of the reasons that patients with antisocial personality disorder frequently slip through the cracks is because mental health, criminal justice, and addictions programs rarely include a discussion with clients about both the diagnosis and its treatment implications. As a therapist or counselor, there are specific steps you can take to engage the client who suffers from both addiction and antisocial personality disorder.

Explain the diagnosis to the client using clear and simple language. This is the beginning of treatment and helps the client avoid becoming part of the revolving-door syndrome where he or she seeks services back and forth between the mental health and addictions disorder systems.

Elicit the client's feelings about what you have just explained about antisocial personality disorder. Show the client the *DSM-IV-TR* criteria for antisocial personality disorder. This puts the client in a position to do a self-diagnosis. The client is more likely to own the diagnosis if he or she makes it.

Discuss the treatment of antisocial personality disorder. Studies reveal that cognitive behavioral therapy can be an effective approach to the treatment of antisocial personality disorder. There are many varieties of cognitive behavioral therapies, including rational emotive therapy, reality therapy, behavior contracting, criminal mind work, and mindfulness (Rotgers and Maniacci 2006; O'Connell and Beyer 2002; Ekleberry 2009). Cognitive distortions (an important component of antisocial personality disorder), which involve feelings of entitlement, a lack of remorse, a lack of empathy, and other criteria discussed earlier, can be changed into rational thinking through cognitive behavioral therapies. When clients change their thinking, their feelings will also change, and these changes ultimately impact their behavior (Corey 2000).

Stress the importance of staying sober, and create a relapse prevention and recovery plan with the client's input. Monitor both relapse triggers and antisocial activity, asking questions at each session to ascertain in which areas the client might benefit from additional support.

Provide recovery support in the client's natural environment. This might involve the use of a recovery coach who has been sober for a number of years, who previously had a lifestyle similar to the client's lifestyle, and who is relatable. See Chapter 6 for additional information.

Provide treatment for other mental disorders. Offer treatment for other mental illnesses that may accompany the antisocial personality disorder, including depression, anxiety disorder, and related disorders.

Help the client develop vocational, educational, and occupational capital. This might involve completion of a GED program, vocational training, job-readiness training, and job placement. In the early stages of recovery, it is helpful for clients with antisocial personality disorder to do the type of work in which they can easily succeed. This often involves solo work in the beginning, such as house painting or being a night watchman. Their personalities often clash with others if there are too many coworkers (Black 1999).

Provide support to the client's family. Explain antisocial personality disorder and addiction to the client's family members and educate them about how the two interact. Discuss with them how to receive their own support, how to protect themselves, and how to be assertive to avoid being victimized by a relative with antisocial personality disorder.

Let the client know that it is possible to decrease antisocial behavior and to recover. When working with clients who have been diagnosed with antisocial personality disorder, it is important to let them know that making progress requires ongoing help, and this diagnosis doesn't give them permission to victimize others. Working with these clients can be quite challenging. They are often mandated to counseling, have co-occurring conditions that lead to resistance, have difficulty with empathy (often a prerequisite to understanding damage done to individuals and society), and they often view their counselors as opponents to be defeated, which can lead to an adversarial relationship. It is also important for counselors to have outlets of self-care when working with these clients.

Research on clients with antisocial personality disorders reveals that one-third make no progress, one-third make some progress (demonstrated by a decrease in antisocial behavior, arrests, drug use, and other defining behaviors), and one-third remit, evidenced by a total discontinuation of antisocial behavior (Black 1999). Many counselors working with clients who have antisocial personality disorders do their interventions when the clients are in their twenties and thirties, often the peak years for criminal activity. It is important to note that a great deal of progress is made when clients reach their forties and beyond (Black 1999). As they get older, they often get tired of the consequences of their behavior: going back and forth to prison can be quite tiresome, and they become more open to change. It is also important that you, the counselor working with these clients, do not take their negativity personally and that you remain hopeful, because many of these clients will make progress after you are no longer working with them. Early interventions can plant the seeds for this later progress.

four

Treating Chemically Dependent Clients Who Have Been Exposed to Trauma

TRAUMA IS A DISORDERED psychic or behavioral state resulting from severe mental or emotional stress or physical injury. Some individuals exposed to trauma go on to develop post-traumatic stress disorder (PTSD), which can put them at risk for substance use disorders (SAMHSA TIP 42 2005). Having a combination of these two disorders can lead to high rates of relapse. Clients with post-traumatic stress disorder attempt to medicate and numb themselves from experiencing the difficult symptoms of this disorder, which include recurrent and intrusive recollections of the traumatic event(s), nightmares, flashbacks, inability to recall all the aspects of the traumatic event, difficulty sleeping, isolation from others, difficulty concentrating, and angry outbursts. Many clients in early recovery who are no longer under the anesthetic influence of alcohol and other drugs re-experience post-traumatic symptoms; this leaves clients vulnerable to continued drug use as a means of coping with these symptoms.

Chemically dependent clients with high rates of exposure to trauma include war veterans, adolescents, gang members, and men and women who have histories of incarceration. While post-traumatic stress disorder is most commonly associated with war and terrorism, trauma can occur anywhere: in the home, at school, in the community, or in prison.

Trauma in the home can include domestic violence, physical and/or verbal abuse, incest, neglect, or abandonment. In a school setting it can include hazing, bully-victim violence, gang violence, rape, racial violence, and school shootings. In the community, violence leading to trauma can be caused by armed robbery, physical and/or sexual assault, gang violence, terrorism, or natural disasters such as hurricanes, earthquakes, floods, and tornadoes.

Prison-related violence causes trauma; verbal abuse, sexual assault, physical attacks, and witnessing violence can all lead to PTSD. Political violence, which includes war and terrorism, is also a source of trauma for anyone exposed to it, and like the other sources it can lead to a diagnosis of PTSD.

Assessing the Effectiveness of Trauma Treatment Programs

With a high rate of exposure to trauma and post-traumatic stress disorder among chemically dependent clients, it is important for chemical-dependence programs to assess their effectiveness in responding to and addressing trauma. A program's ability to address trauma can be seen on a continuum ranging from trauma incapacity to trauma-informed to trauma-competent systems of care. Let's explore each one.

Trauma Incapacity

A "trauma incapacity" program has a staff that lacks the knowledge about how to address trauma. Because of this lack of knowledge, staff may ignore, downplay, or address the client's traumatic experiences inappropriately. In years past, counselors from chemical-dependence programs would accuse clients of defocusing from their addictions treatment if they discussed traumatic experiences they had in the past. This approach would send the message to clients that they should remain silent about their experiences of trauma. This is antitherapeutic and can leave clients vulnerable to slipping through the cracks by isolating themselves and experiencing depression, rage, or psychiatric decompensation or relapse.

Trauma Informed

A trauma-informed program may have some staff who are specialists in addressing trauma. Several staff may have attended specialized training on how to address trauma and are aware of strategies to "do no harm" to clients with trauma histories. These staff may be aware of their own limitations in addressing trauma. They may be the designees on the staff to address trauma and may make referrals for additional help when needed.

Trauma Competent

In a trauma-competent program, the entire organization or system has been trained on how to address trauma while simultaneously helping clients recover from addiction. The staff is also aware of the need to monitor their countertransference reactions when counseling clients exposed to trauma. They have set up systems to address compassion fatigue, the vicarious traumatization that accompanies addressing trauma. This organization is a leader in how to address trauma systematically among clients. Their work is led by research, and they may conduct studies of their own.

It is imperative that addictions programs start to become trauma-competent systems of care. In this preparation, a great deal of emphasis should be placed upon the therapeutic relationship as a primary source of healing client trauma.

Trauma Treatment and the Therapeutic Relationship

The therapeutic relationship is one of the most important aspects of recovery from trauma (Hermann 1997). Counselors strong in empathy, warmth, and genuineness have the capacity to help clients to change and grow (Duncan, Miller, and Sparks 2004). The success of a therapeutic relationship between counselor and client depends on the counselor's understanding of the following ten points.

1. Develop a Positive Counselor-Client Relationship

Recovery from traumatic experiences is most likely to occur when there is a warm relationship between the counselor and the client (Hermann 1997). Clients exposed to trauma often have difficulty trusting; this includes trusting counselors. There are a few actions counselors can take to help facilitate that trust. They include:

- Listening more than you talk.
- Possessing warmth and a nonjudgmental attitude.
- Not backing away from the client's story of trauma through uncomfortable body language or by changing the subject.
- Believing the client.
- Having empathic responses such as "What happened to you was horrible."

- Being comfortable with missing details, as many clients
  do not always remember all the details of traumatic
  experiences

2. Let the Client Set the Pace

As a client exposed to trauma tells his or her story, the client should always be in charge of the pace. This also helps to facilitate rapport. Clients often report that when they were victimized they felt as though they were not in charge. Allowing clients to be in charge of when they share and how much they share can be empowering. Because traumatic experiences are difficult to discuss, clients may not want to talk about the trauma in each session. Allowing this to occur is a perfectly acceptable therapeutic technique.

3. Be a "Moral Witness"

You are a "moral witness." As the client tells his or her story of exposure to trauma, one of your primary responsibilities is to be a good listener and to bear witness to a wrong (Hermann 1997). When you say to the client, "That was wrong" or "What happened to you was horrible," you are validating his or her traumatic experience.

4. Understand That Empowerment Is the Key

One way we empower clients exposed to trauma is to give their experiences a name; for example, "That sounds like rape" or

"It sounds like you experienced domestic violence" are empowering statements. When clients discuss traumatic experiences outside of the counselor's office with others in their lives, these experiences are often minimized or downplayed, or the client is ridiculed and/or blamed for his or her experiences. Consider the client who was sexually abused at age seven, told her parents that she was being sexually abused, and the parents responded by saying: "That never happened. Stop making things up." The client then spends the next thirty years drinking and using drugs heavily to numb the trauma of that experience. Mandated to counseling as a result of driving under the influence of alcohol, the client mentions the traumatic experience that triggered her addiction, which she has not talked about in thirty years. Imagine what might happen if a counselor, who is ill-equipped to address trauma, ignores or minimizes her experience. This could lead to premature termination. When counselors give client experiences a name by saying, "What you're describing sounds like rape," or "That is physical abuse," or "You experienced childhood sexual abuse," the client is more likely to feel heard—sometimes for the first time—and thus empowered.

5. Acknowledge Displaced Rage

Counselors may be the recipients of displaced rage. If a client who was exposed to trauma trusts you, it is common for him or her to displace rage onto you that really belongs to the perpetrator. It is important not to take this rage personally; in fact, clients often display rage where they feel safest. This may be validation of the relationship you have established with the client. It is also helpful to counselors to have outlets where they discuss the myriad feelings they encounter as they are exposed to clients' rage. These outlets can include clinical supervision or working with an outside consultant.

6. Never Back Away from the Story

Counselors must not back away from the story. The elaborate details of trauma experienced by clients can at times be so graphic that the counselor becomes uncomfortable. This could be the details of clients' experiences while on the battlefield, rape, childhood sexual abuse, or gang-related killings. The counselor's discomfort while listening to the details may show in his or her body language or facial expressions, and the client may read this discomfort as it not being okay to tell the story. Seasoned therapists often prepare for the uncomfortable details of a client's story by telling themselves, "I will not be surprised by anything I hear." When repeated on a regular basis this type of mantra can help counselors avoid running away from the stories.

7. Remember the Importance of Boundaries

Boundaries are important. Clients with histories of trauma have often had experiences in which their emotional, physical, and sexual boundaries have been violated by others. They sometimes unconsciously attempt to repeat these inappropriate boundaries with their counselor. The client may unconsciously believe, "If my counselor abuses me, it will prove that I am lovable." It is therefore important that counselors demonstrate healthy physical and emotional boundaries. Many counselors who work with clients exposed to trauma have histories of personal trauma themselves. They are therefore vulnerable to overidentifying with the client's problem and attempting to "rescue" the client. This overinvolvement can also lead to *compassion fatigue*, also known as secondary post-traumatic stress disorder, as a result of internalizing the client's traumatic experiences (Hermann 1997). Good clinical supervision and strategic self-care measures like regular vacations, relaxation, quiet time, daily breaks, and monitoring boundaries can be helpful to counselors.

8. Be Aware of Traumatic Countertransference

Always be aware of traumatic countertransference. Some clients exposed to trauma become perpetrators of trauma themselves. Counselors may find themselves being judgmental as clients tell their stories of the progression from victim to perpetrator. This is a common phenomenon, as many clients exposed to trauma move from victim of sexual abuse to perpetrator, from victimization by childhood sexual abuse to prostitution, or from victim of violence to violent felon. Thus, counselors may find themselves judging the clients for their perpetration and forget that the client's actions were a response to victimization. This can lead to distancing rather than to a relationship and leave clients more vulnerable to slipping through the cracks.

9. Self-Monitor Witness Guilt and Grief Reactions

Be aware of the possibility of "witness guilt" and "grief reactions." As clients tell their stories about being victimized by trauma, some counselors may feel guilty. Other counselors may experience grief as they connect to the clients' stories of loss. It is important for every counselor who works with clients exposed to trauma to have a support network for sharing stirred-up feelings.

10. Address Trauma and Addiction Simultaneously

Be able to address trauma and addiction simultaneously. For many chemically dependent clients, alcohol and drug use serve as an anesthetic to numb them from the shame and/or traumatic stress symptoms that exist as a result of the trauma. Many clients report that as soon as they stop using drugs, the memories, accompanying shame, and traumatic stress symptoms return. This leaves clients vulnerable to relapse. It is imperative for a counselor to partner concretely with a client, laying out a plan for how the client will remain abstinent and deal with traumatic stress symptoms as they emerge.

Trauma Therapy

When a client is in treatment for an addiction and has also suffered a trauma, three phases of trauma treatment need to be addressed: **safety**, **remembering and mourning**, and **reconnection** (Hermann 1997). To keep clients who have been exposed to trauma engaged in treatment, it is important to recognize their vulnerability, which can make them feel unsafe. When feeling unsafe, they tend to create emotional or physical distance, a response that they believe protects them from further harm. As safety is created, clients can feel free to begin the second phase of the treatment—remembering and mourning—the phase in which they share their experiences of victimization and trauma. The goal of the third phase is to help them move forward from a life that has been dampened by trauma.

Safety Phase

Chemically dependent clients in recovery who have been exposed to trauma need to have a plan to feel safe in three areas.

In the home. Helping clients feel safe in their homes involves planning. Clients need options when home feels unsafe because of screaming, verbal abuse, domestic violence, or drugs in the house. It is often helpful to brainstorm how they might feel safer in the home; some of their options might include identifying the safest place in the home to spend time when they are feeling unsafe, or inviting family members who live with them into therapy to discuss safety in the home. Other options might include having a preplanned place to go outside of the home where they feel safer, identifying a supportive network of people to call when feeling unsafe at home, or safe places to take a walk to allow a volatile situation to calm down.

In the community. For a client to feel safe outside of the home, listening to internal cues when in an unsafe environment is important. These internal cues might include tension in the body, increased heart rate, sweating, fear, or the emergence of post-traumatic stress symptoms. Ways to honor these cues might include leaving that environment, having a cell phone ready to dial 911, traveling with members of a support network, taking the safest route to travel, and avoiding the use of alcohol and drugs, especially in public.

In the counselor's office. Your office environment must also feel safe to the client. Counseling techniques such as heavy confrontation can retraumatize clients who have been exposed to trauma (White and Miller 2007). One way to ensure safety in counseling is to make sure that clients are in charge of their self-disclosure. In this process, it is okay for clients to miss details as they tell their stories. Because many traumatized clients do not always remember the details, one experience can stand for many.

Many traumatized clients find it helpful to have a list of people to call when they feel overwhelmed. During counseling, you can help the client generate such a list, which might include phone numbers of a best friend, the safest relative, a counselor, a doctor, the nearest hospital emergency room, a crisis hotline, self-help group members, and others who represent support and safety.

Remembrance and Mourning Phase

In this second phase of trauma treatment, the client feels safe enough to explore his or her story on a deeper level. It is important for counselors to listen to the story and provide emotional support. During this phase, the counselor needs to be comfortable with uncertain details in the stories. As the client expresses feelings connected to what happened to him or her, it is the job of the counselor to normalize those feelings. Remember that testimony can be a healing ritual within itself. It is also helpful to monitor post-traumatic stress disorder symptoms that may emerge as the client does the trauma work and help him or her come up with concrete plans to help manage those symptoms.

Reconnection Phase

In this third phase of treating trauma, clients may need help in developing strategies to avoid being revictimized, as clients exposed to trauma have high rates of revictimization (Hermann 1997). In this phase of trauma treatment, clients learn to stand up for themselves more successfully, revisit old hopes and dreams that were present prior to the trauma, establish new hopes and dreams, create a mission of helping others overcome trauma, and strive to reach their potential.

Dealing with Post-Traumatic
Stress Disorder (PTSD)

To get to the reconnection phase, clients often go through months, even years, of coping with symptoms of post-traumatic stress disorder. Counselors can help clients cope with these symptoms by developing a concrete plan to manage them. Here are some suggestions you as the counselor can give to your client for dealing with debilitating PTSD symptoms like flashbacks and nightmares, and for handling relapse triggers.

HOW TO MANAGE FLASHBACKS AND NIGHTMARES

Chemically dependent clients may experience flashbacks and nightmares as a result of post-traumatic stress disorder. Failure to manage these symptoms can lead the client back to drug use to medicate the pain of the experiences. As a counselor, it is important to remind your clients to:

- Plan in advance what to do if you experience a flashback.
- Call a member of your safety net.
- Ground yourself in the present, using self-talk to remind yourself that the experience is not happening currently.
- Name objects in the environment out loud.
- Hold a safe object, which can be identified during counseling. This object might be a bible or other religious text, a picture of a relative who makes you feel safe, or an artifact given to you by someone you trust.
- Clap your hands or stomp your feet to distract yourself from the flashback.
- Listen to soothing music.
- Say positive affirmations.
- When it comes to preparing yourself for nightmares, decide in advance what you will do if you are awakened by a nightmare connected to your traumatic experiences. As you awaken, remind yourself that you are in your room, that it was a dream, and that you are awake.

Relapse Triggers and Relapse Prevention

Any of the senses can be involved with relapse triggers. One method to prepare clients to address the relapse triggers connected to traumatic stress symptoms and their addiction is to help them divide their triggers into five categories utilizing the senses.

The sense of touch. Holding drug paraphernalia or holding a bottle of alcohol can be a trigger for drug or alcohol use. An unwelcome hug or someone touching your shoulder without permission can trigger a startle response, which is common among individuals with post-traumatic stress disorder.

The sense of smell. Many trauma survivors say that when they were abused, their sense of smell was the most pronounced sense. Smells can sometimes trigger flashbacks; likewise, many chemically dependent clients report that smelling their drug of choice can trigger a craving.

The sense of sight. Seeing perpetrators, people who look like the perpetrators, or seeing acts of violence on television can trigger post-traumatic stress disorder, just as seeing people you once got high with, or seeing drugs or commercials that advertise alcohol can trigger substance cravings.

The sense of hearing. Loud noises, arguments, and other sounds can trigger PTSD flashbacks, and certain songs and language can trigger a craving for drugs.

The sense of taste. Just the taste of alcohol has been known to trigger a full-fledged relapse for chemically dependent clients. Some report that the alcohol contained in over-the-counter mouthwashes can also trigger relapses. For clients who experienced trauma at an event where alcohol was being consumed, the sight and taste of alcohol can also be a trigger.

Clients with addictions and post-traumatic stress disorders have legitimate co-occurring disorders. Both should be considered primary disorders that require focus in order to prevent clients from slipping through the cracks. Counselors can be instrumental in helping clients monitor and manage the unique symptoms and relapse triggers for each disorder. For many years, addictions counselors unfamiliar with how to address trauma have referred clients for ongoing help. While this has been somewhat successful, it is imperative for counselors and the programs they serve to increase competence in addressing trauma and addictions simultaneously to keep clients from slipping through the cracks due to fragmented care.

five

Blending Addictions Counseling with Grief Therapy

THERE IS A LONG, UNWRITTEN PRECEPT in the field of addictions treatment that suggests clients should leave all other problems at the door until they have first dealt with their addictions. As the field matures, we are discovering that many clients cannot recover unless we are able to address a number of problems simultaneously. Grief is often one of these problems, as acute pain around losses seems to resurface as soon as clients stop using. While they were using, clients were able to self-medicate pain by getting high, but once they are abstinent, they may face more than just the addiction; an unforeseen obstacle for these clients is feeling overwhelmed as the pain of unresolved grief surfaces. When they are no longer under the anesthetic influences of drugs or alcohol, they need the help of a counselor to deal with these losses.

Losses to Be Grieved

Counselors must be aware of the numerous losses that clients might grieve, as well as have the skills to help them with the grieving process. Such skills increase the chances that affected clients will not slip through the cracks. In this chapter we will discuss various losses addicted clients might grieve, followed by intervention strategies counselors can use to help them with the grieving process.

Giving Up Alcohol and Drugs

For many clients, alcohol and other drugs have been their most constant companion. Many have discovered that spouses will leave them, relatives will refuse to accept their phone calls, bosses will fire them, but the drugs are always there. Many will be unable to let the drugs go until they mourn the loss of the drugs.

Death of a Child

This is perhaps the most difficult of all losses to grieve. Most people, including counselors, struggle to address this issue. The death of a child leaves parents feeling that a part of themselves has died; they often feel extreme guilt and a unique aloneness. The fact that this loss is often difficult for the bereaved to discuss with their inner circle further exacerbates the pain.

Abortions, Miscarriages, and Stillborn Births

Everyone recognizes the pain that accompanies the loss of a child. Few recognize the pain that accompanies the loss of a fetus or a baby who dies in utero or during childbirth, and these tragedies can be equally devastating. Rarely is there ever a funeral, sympathy, or cards of condolences when one has experienced these losses. There are many women in addiction treatment who have had numerous miscarriages, some exacerbated by their drug use, which increases shame (Sanders 2004). They are often left to grieve these losses alone, unbeknownst to their counselors.

Death of a Parent or Sibling

While the death of a parent can be devastating for anyone, it is particularly difficult for chemically dependent clients, who are often estranged from parents due to their addiction. When their parent dies, it leaves them feeling both grief and guilt about the damage in their relationship, if the relationship was not repaired prior to the parent's death. There are also those chemically dependent clients who are incarcerated because of their addiction; their parent dies, and they are not permitted to attend the funeral. The death of a sibling can also be devastating, coupled with the fact that chemically dependent clients are often estranged from siblings due to harm they have done to their siblings during active addiction. The fact that they may not have been able to make amends to the sibling prior to his or her death may contribute to their grief.

When I was a student intern, I participated in a group in which a client disclosed that he owed money to a drug dealer. The drug dealer came to his house to collect the money. The client's brother, who resembled the client physically, answered the door, and the drug dealer mistakenly shot and killed his brother. The client felt so responsible for his brother's death that each time he attempted abstinence, he would immediately relapse as a result of being overwhelmed with guilt.

Parental Abandonment

This can include physical desertion or emotional unavailability. A clear link was established in the late 1980s between parental abandonment, toxic shame, and addiction (Beattie 1987; Bradshaw 1988). Although the abandonment may have occurred in childhood, this type of pain may still need to be addressed in counseling. Many chemically dependent clients have addictions that are triggered by childhood abandonment, and they often spend years trying to remain abstinent before they ever delve deeply into issues of this abandonment.

Children Placed in the Child Welfare System Due to Parental Addiction

Losing custody of one's children can lead to myriad emotions, including guilt and shame. There are often feelings of hopelessness as a parent wonders if he or she will ever regain custody of the children. Many chemically dependent parents who are in the criminal justice system and have children also experience grief because they miss their children. Both of these issues need to be addressed in counseling.

Failed Relationships, Including Separation and Divorce

Many chemically dependent clients have patterns of unhealthy relationships. It can take clients many years to learn to have healthy relationships. Many bring into treatment a track record of apathy and unresolved grief connected to failed relationships. Many have given up on people and seek companionship with the next pill, fix, hit, or drink. This is an ongoing issue for counselors to be concerned with, as many chemically dependent clients who are married wind up getting divorced during early recovery (Brown, Lewis, and Liotta 2000). Often, the spouse feels the newly sober person is a stranger, not the person he or she married.

Unspeakable Deaths

These are losses that are difficult to discuss and therefore difficult to grieve because they carry a great deal of stigma in our society. Clients may have had relatives or friends who committed

suicide, died of drug overdoses, died from AIDS, or were mur-
dered. Because of the stigma, many clients suffer these losses in
silence (Sanders 2004).

Sexual Abuse

Research reveals that the majority of women who are chemically dependent were either sexually abused as girls or raped as
women (Straussner and Brown 2002). This trauma robs girls and
women of innocence, dignity, self-esteem, choice, and control of
their bodies. Many will suffer an internal death, although they
continue to live externally. Many female clients feel the full pain
of these losses each time they stop using drugs and often return to
drug use to numb the pain. Boys and men fare no better. Because
of the stigma of experiencing sexual abuse as a male, they are
sometimes even more likely to remain silent about their victimization. Suffering in silence can exacerbate shame and increase
the risk of depression and rage. This can serve as a catalyst for
slipping through the cracks.

Loss of Jobs, Status, and Career

These losses can lead to feelings of inadequacy, lower self-
esteem, and an exacerbation of fear. Many chemically dependent
clients have been able to deny their addiction for years with the
mind-set of "I am working, so how can I be an addict?" Both
grief and intense fear can accompany the loss of a job, and unemployed workers often use alcohol and other drugs to "medicate"

these feelings. In the 1980s, as technology replaced human workers in urban America and unemployment rates increased, many communities were fraught with grief, laying the groundwork for a cocaine epidemic to medicate the pain (Sanders 1993).

Loss of Housing

According to noted psychologist Abraham Maslow, our most basic needs from the time we are born are for food, clothing, and shelter (Goble 2004). Many chemically dependent clients share stories about the relationship between loss of housing and slipping through the cracks:

"We had a beautiful house that ended up in foreclosure because of my addiction."

"I could not stand the fact that I left my family homeless. To deal with the pain, I retreated into heavier cocaine use."

"Rock bottom for me was being evicted from my apartment after I lost my job due to my drinking. I went to a shelter and slept there at night, but one of the shelter's rules was that you had to leave the facility during the day. Feelings of uselessness would set in as I wandered the streets. To drown out these feelings, I sought refuge in a bar."

Loss of True Friends

Many clients use the term "associates" for those with whom they spend time during active addiction. "True friends" are relationships that fell apart as the addiction progressed. Although rarely spoken about, many clients mourn the loss of these relationships.

Observing the Deaths of Others

Many clients who have been in wars or those living in neighborhoods where there is extreme violence have witnessed death firsthand. Others have seen people die of drug overdoses or of violence in crack cocaine houses. Many will have symptoms of or actual PTSD, including flashbacks and nightmares, which may need to be addressed along with their addiction.

Grieving Loss

Each client's grief reaction will be uniquely different (Sanders 2004). In the groundbreaking book *On Death and Dying* (1969), Dr. Elisabeth Kübler-Ross outlines the stages of grief: **denial, anger, bargaining, depression,** and **acceptance**. It is significant to note that not all clients go through each stage, nor do they all go through all the stages in order. Some are simply angry as a result of their loss; others stay depressed. Again, grief is individualized. At the same time, it is almost universally true that talking to a nonjudgmental and compassionate person about the loss can be helpful. There is an amazing healing power for clients in simply having someone listen to the stories of their losses (Kolf 1999; Sanders 2004).

There is no single, unique strategy for helping clients cope with their losses. Addiction counselors need many universal skills to help clients deal with the myriad losses they have experienced if counselors are to be effective in helping clients avoid slipping through the cracks. These skills include:

Knowing how to deal with their *own* personal losses. This is an important starting point. When counselors are uncomfortable dealing with their own experiences of loss, the chances that they will ignore or downplay their clients' experiences with loss are increased. I found it was as difficult for staff to talk about loss as it was for clients when I worked in a facility years ago with clients who had dual disorders (mental illness and chemical dependence). During my first day on the job as group therapy supervisor, a client committed suicide, and my first assignment was to process this loss with the remaining clients and staff. The clients expressed increased vulnerability and urges to use drugs to cope with the loss, and they needed staff to process this with them.

One way of becoming more comfortable talking about loss is simply to talk about loss. Simple as this sounds, as one continues to talk about loss, he or she becomes more comfortable with the subject.

Knowledge that each client's grief reaction is uniquely different (Sanders 2004). This is the reason there is no one cookie-cutter approach for helping clients deal with loss. While some clients experience Elisabeth Kübler-Ross's five stages of grief in order—denial, anger, bargaining, depression, and acceptance—some may deal with these stages in a linear fashion, while others may experience them in a more circular fashion (Sanders 2003b).

Recognition of the healing power of simply listening (Kolf 1999; Sanders 2004). In helping clients cope with loss, listening is one of the most important skills that counselors need to possess. When clients are not allowed the opportunity to verbalize feelings connected to their loss, they become more vulnerable to pathological grief reactions and thus to slipping through the cracks (Sanders 2003a). Grief is not a diagnosis from the *Diagnostic and Statistical Manual of Mental Disorders*, nor is it pathological: It is normal. When there is no opportunity to express grief, one becomes more vulnerable to pathological grief reactions, including depression, inability to work and maintain healthy relationships, substance abuse, PTSD, and others as mentioned earlier.

Understanding the losses that accompany sexual trauma (Straussner and Brown 2002). These include the loss of innocence and loss of childhood, as this maltreatment can lead to premature entry into adulthood. As a part of this work with clients who were exposed to sexual trauma, counselors need to help navigate the stages of remembering and mourning that are a part of clients' grief recovery.

Ability to make concrete suggestions to help clients strengthen their recovery plans when they experience loss.

Recognition that issues around previous losses can resurface each year at the anniversary of the loss.

Recognition that tragedies occurring in the larger society can trigger grief reactions in individual clients, including the deaths of revered athletes, movie stars, and politicians, national disasters, terrorism, and war.

Recognition that issues of loss may need to be discussed in individual, group, and family therapy sessions, as these issues can surface in all three milieus.

Helping clients deal with the death of a peer in treatment. Whether this death was caused by medical illness or suicide, this is a particularly difficult loss that creates the need to express feelings, as clients often become close to those with whom they are in recovery.

Recognition of the importance of counselor punctuality. It is important to be on time for therapy sessions, so as to avoid clients' feelings of abandonment. The great majority of chemically dependent clients have issues of childhood abandonment. In many instances this abandonment can be the precursor to substance use (Brown et al. 2000).

Understanding the relationship between relapse and loss. Regardless of whether the loss was the death of a parent, divorce, job layoff, eviction, death of one's child or a pet, clients will experience grief. There is a strong relationship between unexpressed grief and relapse (Sanders 2003a).

Helping Clients Remember Rather Than Forget Their Losses

Sigmund Freud described a normal grieving period as lasting six months to a year, and everything beyond a year was considered pathological. (Sanders 2004). Today it is believed that grief is actually about remembering rather than forgetting losses. As stated earlier, clients tend to attempt to bury the pain of their losses, which can resurface in self-destructive manners. There are many suggestions counselors can make to help clients remember rather than try to forget/bury their feelings of grief. These include:

Keeping memories alive. Helping clients identify strategies to help them keep memories alive, such as telling stories about their loved one, visiting gravesites, weaving interests of the loved one into their own lives, or keeping a place for a loved one during ceremonies.

Journaling. Clients grieving the loss of a loved one can write about their fondest memories, ways in which their loved one affected their lives, and what they remember most. If the loss was of something rather than of someone, journaling can help relieve stress and provide an outlet for feelings of grief.

Turning grief into purpose. The organization Mothers Against Drunk Drivers (MADD) was founded by a mother who lost her child to an accident caused by a drunk driver. Counselors can help their clients identify ways of turning grief into purpose, which is empowering.

Joining grief support groups. The relationship between relapse and loss is a substantial component of the revolving-door syndrome, and the ability to make concrete suggestions to help clients strengthen their recovery plans when they experience loss is a skill every counselor should strive to attain. When a client is feeling overwhelmed by loss, there is a greater chance for that client to terminate therapy prematurely and slip through the cracks.

Terminating Therapy

While the counselor/client relationship during treatment is key to a successful addiction recovery, it is also necessary to recognize the importance of a good counselor/client termination. An effective termination can be the most beneficial aspect of the therapeutic experience for clients. This may be the first time that some clients have had the opportunity to deal with a loss or separation without denial, fleeing, or using drugs.

Generally speaking, the longer the relationship between counselor and client, the more time will be required to terminate. This process can be initiated with the counselor bringing up the issue of termination after the treatment goals have been met by asking the client, "How do you think things will be when we are no longer meeting?" The counselor should realize that clients often go through a number of phases before totally accepting termination, similar to the stages of grief, including denial, anger, sadness, and release. A critical skill is to allow clients to express their feelings openly in each stage. There are a number of strategies a counselor can use in each stage to help clients avoid slipping through the cracks.

Denial stage. When clients are in the denial stage of termination, they will often regress, acting in ways they were acting prior to starting counseling, because they fear termination. It is important for the counselor to identify this behavior and then ask the client, "Is that an issue for you? Can we talk about that?"

Anger. When clients are in the anger stage, they are vulnerable to leaving counseling prematurely. The message they want to send is, "I will leave you before you leave me." It is important to allow clients in this stage to express their anger, to normalize their anger, and to avoid getting angry with them, as their anger directed toward you is not personal; rather, it is a response to termination.

Sadness. It is often valuable to help clients express their sad feelings, as this is part of the grieving process and often a necessary step before the final stage of termination.

Release. There are many tasks for this final stage of termination. Consider the following actions:

- Allow clients to reminisce and review the gains they made in counseling.

- Discuss measures clients will take to maintain sobriety to avoid slipping through the cracks.

- Discuss your working relationship. This can begin by asking the client, "What was it like to work with me?" This is a significant phase of termination, because many clients have histories of relationships ending badly, such as with police being called, with a fight, with fleeing, or with drug use. This teaches clients to deal with the pain of termination by talking.

- Final good-bye. During this phase, it is often helpful to express your sincere belief in the client's ability to succeed, as well as letting him or her know of your availability should he or she require services in the future.

When the termination stage of counseling is handled well, a client leaves with the belief that he or she can build other relationships in the future without fearing the end (loss) of the relationship before it begins. He or she will have acquired a skill set that not only allows for dealing with grief in the past but offers tools for dealing with potential pitfalls and losses in the future as well.

six

Recovery Management and the Use of Recovery Coaches

ECOVERY MANAGEMENT IS an emerging approach for treating addiction with methods similar to the treatment of other chronic and progressive illnesses such as cancer and diabetes (White, Kurtz, and Sanders 2006). There is evidence that substance use disorders, particularly dependence, are chronic illnesses (White and McClellan 2008). Yet, we have historically treated them as though they are acute illnesses, using a prescribed regimen of three days of detox, fourteen days of residential treatment, three weeks of intensive outpatient treatment, and so on. According to the American Medical Association, chronic illnesses are considered in remission after five years of stability. But there are very few five-year chemical-dependence programs in the country; this leaves most clients with an inadequate service dose. What is needed to improve long-term recovery results is a plan for addiction recovery management.

Successful recovery management—that is, long-term and ongoing support—is often anchored in the client's natural environment. This is a significant concept, because the great majority of treatment centers across the country often have only one or two contacts with clients following discharge. As part of the recovery-management model, the use of recovery coaches with adults is achieving promising results in helping clients with early recovery and beyond (GLATTC Bulletin 2005). For example, in Connecticut, Phil Valentine is director of a recovery support services volunteer program. He has recruited 150 recovering volunteers who visit treatment centers and offer to call clients by telephone once a week for twelve weeks (ninety days) to offer recovery support after discharge.

What Is a Recovery Coach?

A recovery coach is often the person who serves as a guide in supporting individual recovery. A coach's primary credential is not possession of an advanced degree; it is the fact that he or she has "been there." This coach is a lifestyle consultant whose individual story is proof that recovery is possible. In addition to

READER/CUSTOMER CARE SURVEY

HEFG

We care about your opinions! Please take a moment to fill out our online Reader Survey at **http://survey.hcibooks.com**.

As a **"THANK YOU"** you will receive a **VALUABLE INSTANT COUPON** towards future book purchases

as well as a **SPECIAL GIFT** available only online! Or, you may mail this card back to us.

(PLEASE PRINT IN ALL CAPS)

First Name		MI.		Last Name

Address			City

State	Zip	Email

1. Gender
☐ Female   ☐ Male

2. Age
☐ 8 or younger
☐ 9-12   ☐ 13-16
☐ 17-20   ☐ 21-30
☐ 31+

3. Did you receive this book as a gift?
☐ Yes   ☐ No

4. Annual Household Income
☐ under $25,000
☐ $25,000 - $34,999
☐ $35,000 - $49,999
☐ $50,000 - $74,999
☐ over $75,000

5. What are the ages of the children living in your house?
☐ 0 - 14   ☐ 15+

6. Marital Status
☐ Single
☐ Married
☐ Divorced
☐ Widowed

7. How did you find out about the book?
(please choose one)
☐ Recommendation
☐ Store Display
☐ Online
☐ Catalog/Mailing
☐ Interview/Review

8. Where do you usually buy books?
(please choose one)
☐ Bookstore
☐ Online
☐ Book Club/Mail Order
☐ Price Club (Sam's Club, Costco's, etc.)
☐ Retail Store (Target, Wal-Mart, etc.)

9. What subject do you enjoy reading about the most?
(please choose one)
☐ Parenting/Family
☐ Relationships
☐ Recovery/Addictions
☐ Health/Nutrition
☐ Christianity
☐ Spirituality/Inspiration
☐ Business Self-help
☐ Women's Issues
☐ Sports

10. What attracts you most to a book?
(please choose one)
☐ Title
☐ Cover Design
☐ Author
☐ Content

TAPE IN MIDDLE; DO NOT STAPLE

BUSINESS REPLY MAIL
FIRST-CLASS MAIL PERMIT NO 45 DEERFIELD BEACH, FL

POSTAGE WILL BE PAID BY ADDRESSEE

Health Communications, Inc.
3201 SW 15th Street
Deerfield Beach FL 33442-9875

FOLD HERE

Comments

being in recovery, recovery coaches are often indigenous healers who reach out to clients in neighborhoods they are familiar with and are comfortable navigating. The recovery coach differs from a sponsor in that a sponsor primarily supports one pathway to recovery (usually the 12-step approach), while the recovery coach is charged with supporting multiple pathways to recovery. He or she is not a therapist; there is no probing, uncovering of unconscious material, delving into the interactions between the id and superego, or making diagnoses. Instead, he or she provides ongoing recovery *support* in the client's natural environment (White, Kurtz, and Sanders 2006).

Studies show that 80 percent of clients who relapse do so within ninety days of completing treatment (GLATTC Bulletin 2005), but with the recovery coach model like the one adopted in Connecticut, research reveals that 80 percent of these clients are still sober at the ninety-day mark (White 2008).

Recovery Management in Action

There are three phases of recovery management, each of which can be enhanced by using recovery coaches.

Phase 1: Pretreatment Recovery Support

Research reveals that 75 percent of chemically dependent clients will never enter addictions treatment in their lifetimes (White, Kurtz, and Sanders 2006). Instead, they often wind up in hospitals to address medical complications caused by their drug use, in prisons, or in psychiatric institutions (White, Kurtz, and Sanders 2006). This phase often involves the use of recovery coaches who engage clients in their natural environments prior to treatment, with the goal of motivating them to seek help for their addiction.

Phase 2: In-Treatment Recovery Support

Approximately 50 percent of chemically dependent clients leave treatment prematurely (GLATTC Bulletin 2005). A promising approach is one used by Phil Valentine, executive director of Connecticut Community for Addiction Recovery, who uses volunteer recovery coaches to connect with clients while they are in primary treatment. Post-treatment research reveals that 80 percent of these individuals are still abstinent ninety days after leaving treatment. The frequency with which coaches interact with clients varies from program to program. In some programs, recovery coaches may have one or two contacts while the client is in inpatient treatment. If the client is receiving outpatient services, he or she may meet with the recovery coach once a week and the therapist once a week, with each professional having a different role. The therapist may address issues of trauma, family therapy, co-occurring disorders, and so forth, while the recovery coach might help clients get connected to resources in the community, make effective linkages to mutual aid groups of recovery, help them stay sober, and navigate stressors in their communities between therapy appointments. Recovery coaches, who may not be trained in evidence-based practices, are often taught basic communication and relationship-building skills.

Phase 3: Post-Primary Treatment Recovery Support

With this level of engagement, recovery coaches work with clients in their natural environments to help them deal with the myriad challenges they face in their efforts to stay sober. These include family conflict, unemployment, cravings to use drugs, peer pressure to use drugs, pressure from bill collectors, the challenges involved in efforts to disengage from subcultures of addiction, and relationship issues. Clients requiring the greatest recovery support postdischarge include those with the highest problem severity and lowest recovery capital, which means they have few internal and external assets that aid in recovery efforts (White and Cloud 2008). Recovery coaches can provide a range of supports to these clients in early recovery, including help with reintegration into the family; social, vocational, and occupational support; transportation; help with problem solving and decision making; and help with both disengagement from drug cultures and linking into communities of recovery.

Recovery Management, Recovery Coaches, and Specific Treatment Groups

Counselors can facilitate the use of recovery management and recovery coaches whenever a client is at risk for slipping through the cracks, but for two specific groups—rural methamphetamine users and adolescents—this method appears to be an especially effective treatment option.

Battling Methamphetamine Use in Rural America

The use of methamphetamine is ravaging rural America, causing a great deal of damage to the user and to society (California Department of Alcohol and Drug Programs 2007). The keynote speaker for an addictions conference I recently attended in a southwestern state was an attorney general. This was striking to me; in the twenty-seven years I have been an addictions counselor, this was the first time I had attended a conference where a law enforcement agent was the keynote speaker. Keynote speakers at conferences are usually academics, researchers, seasoned addictions speakers, or administrators from the Center for Substance Abuse Treatment (CSAT) or the National Institute on Drug Abuse (NIDA). This man's appearance was unusual because states' attorneys are not generally a part of addictions conferences.

The attorney general's appearance indicated that the use of this particular drug created a state of emergency (California Department of Alcohol and Drug Programs 2007). One of the most important points he made in his address was that methamphetamine use was the number-one drug, legal, public health, and child welfare problem in his state.

Many authors (Sim et al. 2002; Hoffman and Lefkowitz 1993; Gonzales et al. 2006; Holton 2001) have described the impact and effects of methamphetamine. For the user, these include: paranoia; depression; extreme anxiety; hallucinations that often produce symptoms resembling paranoid schizophrenia; suicidal ideation; suicide; memory impairment that resembles the early stages of Alzheimer's disease; legal problems; and health problems, including increased risk for heart attacks, convulsions, strokes, hepatitis C, and dental decay. Methamphetamine use also damages the communities in which it is manufactured. Statistics from the California Department of Alcohol and Drug Programs in 2007 showed an increase in crime and violence as well as contamination of the environment. For every pound of methamphetamine manufactured, approximately six pounds of toxic waste are deposited into backyards, parks, roadsides, motels, and local water supplies. There is also a risk of poisoning, burns, lung irritation, organ damage, and cancer for both the users and exposed bystanders.

One of the most vulnerable groups affected by methamphetamine use is children. Not only is there deterioration in family relationships as the parents focus primarily on obtaining and using the drug, but the health of the children is also at risk if they are in proximity while the drug is being manufactured or used. Law enforcement commonly deals with meth use by staging raids, and these raids have led to the coining of the term *meth orphans*, referring to children brought into the child welfare system. Recovery management, specifically the use of recovery coaches, can be instrumental in helping methamphetamine users recover in their natural environments and may provide needed resources for children who are affected by their parents' drug use.

In spite of the fact that methamphetamine use is an ongoing crisis in rural America, meth users accounted for only 8 percent of all treatment admissions in the United States in 2009 (SAMHSA 2009a). Their symptomatology (that is, apathy, feelings of depression, isolation, involvement with destructive peer groups, and physical deterioration) makes it difficult for methamphetamine addicts to reach out for help (California Department of Alcohol and Drug Programs 2007). One administrator for the CSAT indicated that if clients were not coming in, they would have to go out and get them.

Methamphetamine addicts have biopsychosocial challenges that make completing primary treatment even more difficult than it is for other addicts. These challenges include memory deficit, intense cravings, depression, and heightened emotionality and anger. One study indicated that 50 percent of methamphetamine addicts drop out of inpatient treatment prematurely, and 70 percent drop out of outpatient treatment (California Department of Alcohol and Drug Programs 2007).

Methamphetamine users face many difficulties upon discharge that make staying sober a challenge (Olbert 2000). They are more likely to be under criminal justice supervision than are other clients, making it difficult for them to secure employment. They struggle with intense cravings that often lure them back to active addiction. For approximately ninety days after discontinuing use, meth addicts often struggle with depression and anhedonia (difficulty achieving pleasure). They may have difficulty with memory and often suffer from cognitive impairment. The use of recovery coaches as part of a recovery management strategy can be helpful here, as many recovery coaches faced similar challenges in the early stages of their own recovery. These coaches can provide emotional recovery support by explaining some of the challenges clients will experience in early recovery and normalizing those experiences.

Rarely in modern history has a drug had such a stronghold in rural America in such a short period. Even speed (in the 1960s) and crack cocaine (in the 1980s) didn't become the powerhouses that methamphetamines have become. Recovery management offers clients, families, and communities a great deal of recovery support before, during, and after primary treatment. Recovery coaches can provide social recovery support, such as spending time with methamphetamine users who are attempting to disengage from methamphetamine subcultures, and transportational recovery support, as services in rural America are often difficult to navigate. In some programs, the recovery coaches actually pick clients up in a van or a bus. While transporting them, they may also discuss challenges clients are facing in their recovery. Recovery coaches can be instrumental in helping clients access occupational recovery support—that is, supporting clients as they seek gainful employment, helping to steer them into job readiness programs, and coaching them as to how to answer questions on job applications about previous arrests. And coaches can offer emotional recovery support, by providing compassion to clients as they face challenges in recovery.

Adolescents and Recovery Coaches

Adolescents are often difficult to engage in addictions treatment because they do not believe they have a problem (Higgins et al. 2008). Their mind-set is, "I smoke marijuana every day and I can still run the 100-yard dash in eight seconds. How can I be an addict?" Adolescents are also difficult to engage because they are in the last developmental stage prior to adulthood. An adolescent's primary goal is to pull away from adult authority of every sort, including counselors, and that puts the adolescent at risk for recidivism.

Thus far, most of the emphasis on recovery management and recovery coaching has focused on adult populations. Can adolescents benefit from a recovery coach? I believe they can, for a number of reasons.

- The majority of adolescents with substance use disorders have co-occurring conditions requiring recovery support to help manage the multiple stresses (Riggs and Davies 2002).
- Navigating relationships with peers can be a major relapse trigger for adolescents (Liddle and Rowe 2005).
- Often, a combination of risk factors exists that increase the chances of relapse and incarceration, including living in high-risk communities where there are high crime and poverty rates. (Mayeda and Sanders 2007).
- Substance use disorders are "family illnesses" (Sanders 2003). In a 2007 focus group commissioned by the

Illinois Division of Alcoholism and Substance Abuse of adolescents with substance-use disorders, *problems within their families* was named the number-one stressor for them when leaving treatment.

- Academic problems are particularly stressful for adolescents with substance use disorders (Liddle and Rowe 2005). Many have been expelled or have dropped out of school because of problems caused by their substance use.

- In many communities, it is seen as "cool" for adolescents to get high, and many teens believe that almost everyone gets high, making it difficult to stay sober in such an environment.

- Like adults, the great majority of adolescents who relapse do so within the first three months after leaving treatment (Mayeda and Sanders 2007).

With adult populations, recovery coaches are often adults who have been sober for a year or longer. Who qualifies to serve as a recovery coach for teens? Is the ideal coach an adolescent who has been sober for at least one year, an adolescent who has been sober for two or more years, a young adult in recovery who can share his or her experience in recovery, an adult in his or her thirties (recovering or not), a trained psychotherapist, or someone else? This question was posed to teens in the Illinois focus group mentioned earlier.

The consensus was that an ideal recovery coach would be a

young adult who is not older than twenty-five and who has two or more years of recovery. Someone in this age group is young enough to understand adolescents' concerns, yet experienced in recovery and someone to whom they can relate. When asked what they considered an "older" recovery support specialist, the teens said "anyone over thirty-five." They went on to state that they would be receptive to receiving recovery support from "older adults" if they were sincere, willing to be honest, and had a "good vibe."

The focus group mentioned was conducted with just one group of adolescents. It is necessary to continue to explore the question of who qualifies to be a recovery coach with adolescents. If adolescents are well matched with a recovery coach, the chance that they will stay engaged and not slip through the cracks is increased. Questions to explore include:

- What is the appropriate age for a coach?
- How important is gender pairing?
- Does the recovery coach need to understand the young person's culture?
- What should a coach's sobriety status be? (Must the coach be a recovering person?)
- Because many adolescents communicate today via technology (cell phones, text messaging, social media), does the coach need to be technology savvy?
- Would adolescents be more comfortable with different

language, such as "peer recovery support specialist," or a similar term? Should the recovery support specialist even be called a "coach"?

- What knowledge do recovery coaches need about adolescents in order to be effective? How much formal training should be involved, and where should that training be obtained?

- Should we use an individualized approach in pairing youth with recovery coaches, with the youth having the final say?

- Is special training necessary because these clients are not adults?

Recovery coaches need a solid foundation in their own recovery if they are going to be helpful to the clients they coach. Recovery coaching is not a substitute for their own therapy or for their own need to receive recovery support. Recovery coaches often benefit from supervisors who help them set and maintain appropriate boundaries for clients and help them monitor burnout so they can remain therapeutic change agents.

Recovery management is an emerging model, geared toward helping clients remain sober in their natural environment. The Center for Substance Abuse Treatment (CSAT) has funded programs to provide peer-based recovery support services throughout the United States. These recovery support services are being provided in hospital settings, Native American reservations, schools, and urban and rural environments with a range of client populations, including the aforementioned methamphetamine users and adolescents. There are more than 800 scientific studies outlining the impact of peers helping peers recover (White 2009).

From the Washingtonian movement of the early 1800s, where recovering alcoholics inspired active drinkers with the stories of their recoveries, the Alcoholics Anonymous of the 1930s, where individuals in recovery learned that one of the best ways to maintain their own sobriety was to help others, through the peer-based recovery management movement of today, individuals in recovery have a long history of helping each other with abstinence (White 2009).

seven

Motivational Interviewing

A THERAPIST OR COUNSELOR WHO is working with an at-risk client has a primary goal of facilitating changes that will allow the client to maintain sobriety. Motivational interviewing is an approach designed to help the client build a commitment and reach a decision to change. Research reveals that this approach, developed by Dr. William Miller in the early 1990s, is effective for clients who are difficult to reach and who may be ambivalent about changing or are reluctant to do so. (For books and videos on the techniques and the application process for becoming part of a motivational interviewing network of trainers (MINT), visit www.motivationalinterview .com).

Goals of Motivational Interviewing

Motivational interviewing is a client-centered, directive method that integrates the person-centered approach of Carl Rogers, one of the founders of the humanistic approach to psychology (Miller and Rollnick 2002). It is nonconfrontational and is a revolutionary approach to working with clients who have substance use disorders.

The goals of motivational interviewing include helping the client to:

- make the argument for why he or she should change;
- become the expert on why he or she should change;
- discover more reasons to discontinue harmful behavior than to continue;
- examine whether or not he or she should stop the behavior; and
- make the argument for change.

Asking directive questions of a client is part of what separates motivational interviewing from a purely client-centered approach. With both approaches, the client leads and does more talking than the counselor. With motivational interviewing, the counselor asks directive questions, such as, "Although you say that alcohol is not a problem for you, are there times that you do believe it is a problem?" or "If you continue to smoke cocaine, where do you think your life will be in five years?" These types of questions guide clients to examine their drug use, its impact, and whether they should continue to use.

The Five Principles of Motivational Interviewing

There are five principles that guide motivational interviewing:

1. Express empathy
2. Develop discrepancies
3. Avoid arguing
4. Roll with resistance
5. Support self-efficacy

Let's look at each of these principles in more detail.

Express Empathy

An early task of motivational interviewing is to build a client-centered, positive working relationship with the client. One way counselors can begin to achieve this is by using empathy. Being empathetic in motivational interviewing means two things: total acceptance and reflection of feelings.

Total Acceptance

Accepting the client as a human being does not necessarily mean accepting all the client's behavior. When counselors accept their clients as human beings, clients will often feel this acceptance and become less resistant. For example, you are working with a client who stole from his mother to support his drug habit. As a counselor, you have a strong negative reaction to this, and one way you may be able to accept the client is by separating the client's behavior from his being. You acknowledge to yourself that the client's behavior was inappropriate, wrong, and against the law, but the person you are working with is seeking your help. By separating the behavior from the person's being, you may be able to continue working with him.

Reflection of Feelings

By reflecting the feeling content of statements made by clients, counselors are better able to demonstrate empathy, and the client feels understood. Examples include, "It sounds as though you feel angry," and "It sounds as though you feel scared." Reflection of feelings helps difficult-to-reach clients feel understood, decreases their defensiveness, and increases the chance that they will be willing to examine whether or not they should make changes.

Develop Discrepancies

The counselor may use techniques to elicit discrepancies, but ultimately the client has to feel the discrepancy internally to create change. Clients are more likely to change if there is a discrepancy between a previous or current goal and a current behavior. There are different types of discrepancies:

A discrepancy between what a client says and what he or she does. In this case, a counselor might say, "On the one hand, you say you want to stop drinking, and at the same time, you've told me that you spend each evening in bars."

A discrepancy between what a client does and an important value. The counselor might say, "You say that you always wanted to be a good son, and yet, you've told me on several occasions that you have stolen from your mother to support your drug habit."

A discrepancy between a client's behavior and an important goal. The counselor could say, "You told me that you've always wanted to race in the Olympics, and at the same time, you smoke two packs of cigarettes a day."

This approach, which produces less resistance in clients than the use of heavy confrontation (SAMHSA 2008), creates an internal confrontation.

Avoid Arguing

Arguing makes clients defensive, and they are less likely to continue to engage in counseling. When clients are defensive, they are less likely to examine whether or not they should change.

Roll with Resistance

It is important to roll with or join resistance rather than oppose it. This can be accomplished in a number of ways:

Acknowledging the resistance. For example, the counselor might say, "You seemed uncomfortable when I began talking about your heroin use."

Emphasizing personal choice. The counselor might say, "It's up to you to decide if you want to live in a half-way house."

Siding with the negative. The counselor could say, "It sounds as though you may not be ready to look at this issue at this time."

Shifting the focus. The counselor might say, "Let's go back to what we were talking about before I asked you about your drug use."

Support Self-Efficacy

Showing genuine enthusiasm about any steps the client has already made toward changing increases the chances that the client will be excited about his or her own change and may motivate the client to continue changing.

The Use of Motivational Interviewing in Early Sessions

An important step in initial sessions is to create a climate in which clients will feel comfortable enough to examine whether or not they should change. Clients need support rather than heavy confrontation as they struggle to make an argument for whether or not they should change. To facilitate this process, counselors and therapists can use the specific strategies discussed below.

Establishing a Client-Centered Relationship

This involves listening more than talking, asking opened-ended questions, paraphrasing, summarizing, reflecting the client's feelings, and placing the emphasis on the client as the director of his or her plan. This automatically reduces resistance to counseling (Rosengren 2009).

Providing Education

When clients are reluctant to change because they do not believe they have a problem, a counselor or therapist can provide simple education by stating facts, providing pamphlets, or watching short videos with clients. These educational strategies can sometimes help clients recognize that there is a need to change (Valesquez et al. 2001).

Discussing the Results of an Alcohol/Drug Assessment

When an alcohol or drug assessment proves that a client has a substance use disorder, going over those results with the client is often helpful. By modeling the compassionate style of a caring physician instead of that of a prosecuting attorney, the client feels he or she has a partner instead of an accuser who charges: "I caught you! You're an addict!"

Discussing the Results of a Medical Exam

Using the style of a caring physician (meaning nonaccusatory and compassionate), going over the results of a medical examination can help clients reach the decision that there is a problem that needs to be addressed. For example, the counselor might say, "Your medical exam reveals that you have gout, hepatitis C, and fatty liver. These conditions are often associated with heavy drinking." Such a statement can be instrumental in increasing the client's urgency to do something about his or her problem before his or her health is destroyed by alcohol or drug use.

Facilitating Values Clarification

When clients discover a discrepancy between an important value and their behavior, they have a clearly defined reason to make a change. Consider statements such as these:

Counselor: "You said that honesty has always been important to you, and you've told me that you've lied to loved ones in order to hide your drinking," or, **Counselor:** "What are the five things that you value most? What impact has your drinking had on those values?"

The internal discomfort clients can feel as they realize that a current behavior conflicts with an important value serves as an internal confrontation.

Role Clarification

During this process, clients begin to understand the impact of their current behavior on important roles such as parent, employee, employer, student, husband, wife, clergy, friend, sister, or brother. A counselor might encourage this by saying, "What are your seven most important roles? What impact, if any, has your drug use had on your ability to do well in these roles?"

The effectiveness of motivational interviewing in early sessions is also contingent on knowing what to avoid. Some of these missteps include:

Prematurely Deciding the Focus of Counseling

Many difficult-to-reach clients have multiple problems. When counselors decide too early which problems to focus on, clients become more resistant to counseling for several reasons:

- Many clients come to counseling believing they do not have a problem that needs to be changed. When counselors decide the focus of counseling too early, clients become resistant because they have not acknowledged that they have a problem that needs to change.

- Deciding the focus of counseling creates distance, because the client is not in the driver's seat of the change process.

Talking Too Much About Change or Assuming Client Is Ready to Change

As stated earlier, a goal of motivational interviewing is to help clients make the argument as to why they should change. When counselors spend too much time early in the counseling relationship talking about change, this can increase client resistance. At this early stage, many clients have not yet acknowledged the problem; therefore, talking about change leads to resistance.

Confrontation

Research reveals a strong relationship between counselor confrontation and a client's premature termination, and between counselor confrontation and clients continuing to drink. No research proves that heavy confrontation gets clients sober (Miller and Rollnick 2002). In fact, studies with chemically dependent women reveal that confrontation can retraumatize those clients who have histories of exposure to trauma (White and Miller 2007).

Being an Expert

Clients aren't helped by a counselor who "knows it all" and can recite a dozen reasons why change is necessary. The goal is to help the client become the expert on why he or she should change.

Overcoming Ambivalence

Proponents of motivational interviewing believe clients are more likely to be *ambivalent* about whether or not they should discontinue their drug use and other behavior than to be in *denial* about their addictions. In other words, a part of the client wants to continue to drink, and another part wants to quit; a part of the client wants to continue selling crack-cocaine, and another part doesn't.

A major goal of motivational interviewing is to help clients discover more reasons to discontinue harmful behavior than to continue (Rosengren 2009). With this approach, the counselor walks alongside the client instead of leading the client in the change process. The counselor helps the client make the argument for why he or she should change (Rollnick, Miller, and Butler 2008). Once the decision to change has been reached, the counselor helps the client take action and sustain the change. There are a number of useful strategies to try to help clients eliminate their ambivalence.

Speak to Both Sides of the Ambivalence

Far too often, counselors discuss why the client should give up certain behaviors while ignoring the client's ambivalence. In some instances, the more counselors push for one side, the more the client clings to the other side. An example of speaking to both sides of the ambivalence might be: "Can you tell me about the part of you that wants to continue gambling?" and then, "Can you tell me about the part of you that wants to stop gambling?"

Create a Balance Sheet

Have the client draw a line down the middle of a sheet of paper. On the left side, he or she can list all the reasons to continue the current behavior; on the right side, he or she can list all the reasons to stop it. With this cognitive exercise, clients are able to see and examine all the positives and negatives of a current behavior.

Solicit Feedback from Loved Ones

Clients are often unaware of the impact their behavior has on their loved ones. When they receive honest feedback, it becomes harder for them to ignore how problematic their behavior really is.

Honor the Four Laws of Ambivalence

According to Miller and Rollnick (2002), the four laws of ambivalence are the laws of paradox, freedom, conflict, and "I heard what I said."

The Law of Paradox

Few people wish to be told what to do. When a counselor chooses one side of the client's ambivalence—for example, "You need to quit smoking cigarettes"—a client will often choose the other side of the ambivalence: "I'll continue smoking cigarettes." This law reminds the counselor of the importance of speaking to both sides of the ambivalence.

The Law of Freedom

Clients will often make bad choices if they feel that their personal freedom is being taken away. Logic would dictate that every client who received a DUI would go to the court-ordered remedial education classes if that was the way to reinstate a driver's license; yet many will not if they feel that it is not their own choice. To honor this principle, counselors can give choices to clients, even those who are mandated. For example, a counselor might say: "The judge has mandated you to have this assessment, and I'm planning to refer you for ongoing counseling. I have three referral sources. You can decide which one to use."

The Law of Conflict

Conflict occurs when the counselor and client have dissimilar or incompatible goals. To avoid this conflict, it is helpful for counselors to examine their own goals. Early in my own career as a drug counselor, my goal was to help all my clients stop using. Many of them wanted to continue using drugs and were using rehab as a temporary vacation from drug use. I discovered that when I worked with clients whose goals were to continue using drugs, and my goal was to get them to stop, we had a great deal of conflict. When I changed my goal to being the best drug counselor I could be, I noticed that there was less conflict in our relationships. A major goal of motivational interviewing is for the *client* to examine whether or not he or she should stop the behavior.

The Law of "I heard what I said."

When clients choose one side of their ambivalence—for example, stating "I'm not an alcoholic"—they hear what they say and will often cling to it—not because they believe it, but because they said it. This law is more likely to be activated when counselors diagnose clients prematurely, use confrontational techniques, argue with clients, or meet resistance with resistance. Once a person's mind is made up ("I'm not an alcoholic"), he or she can spend many years defending this position. I have known clients who were diagnosed with schizophrenia the first day they met their psychiatrist, and then spent the next fifteen years proving to themselves that they were not schizophrenic by refusing to take psychiatric medication.

Ask Directive Questions

The goal of directive questions is to help clients make the argument for change. Asking directive questions of a client is part of what separates motivational interviewing from a purely client-centered approach, and is one of the most important aspects of motivational interviewing. Here are some examples of directive questions:

- "What are the advantages and disadvantages of continuing to sell drugs?"

- "What was your life like before you started using methamphetamines and being a member of a motorcycle gang?" (Looking back on one's life can often create an internal confrontation. Clients can see a discrepancy between where they wanted to be and where they are currently.)

- "If you stopped using methamphetamines and you left the motorcycle gang, what, if anything, would you have to look forward to?" or "If you stop using drugs, where do you think you will be in five years?" (A positive vision for the future can sometimes be instrumental in helping clients decide that they need to change a current behavior.)

- "If you continue to use heroin, what is the most extreme scenario?"

- "What is the worst possible outcome if you continue with a life of crime?"

- "What are the best possible outcomes if you stop drinking?"

Clients Who Are Hesitant to Change

There are a number of reasons why clients who are motivated to change may be hesitant to do so. But regardless of the reason, there are a number of strategies that may help further motivate clients who are hesitant to change:

Identify the Reasons for Hesitation; Remove the Barriers

For example, among chemically dependent women who are thinking of entering treatment, concern about child care while they are in treatment may be an issue. A counselor might ask, "If I could refer you to a treatment center that has child care on the premises, would you be willing to enter that program?" Among other groups, another barrier may be poverty. In this case, the question could be, "If I could refer you to a program that has a bus shuttle service or provides bus tokens, would that be attractive to you?" Concern about distance may also be a barrier, so the appropriate question could be, "If I were able to refer you to a program within three blocks of your home, how likely would you be to enter that program?" If language or cultural barriers are the roadblock, asking the client "Would you be interested in receiving services in English or Spanish? I can refer you to either," can open the door.

Provide a Menu of Options

Giving clients choices can motivate them to pursue the change process. Examples of how to offer the client a menu of options include asking these types of question:

- "We have a number of therapy groups for you to choose from. Why don't you look over our list and tell us the ones you would like to attend?"

- "I have a list of three therapists who specialize in the problem you want to address. Would you be interested in talking to each one to find out which one you would be more comfortable working with?"

- "Would you prefer to go to counseling near your home or place of employment?"

- "What is the best time of day for you to receive counseling services?"

Increase Client Confidence in Their Ability to Change

Some clients have the motivation to change but lack confidence in their ability *to* change. Several strategies that have proved successful in increasing the client's confidence in his or her ability to change include:

Utilizing the Confidence Ruler

A counselor or therapist asks a client, "On a scale of 1 to 10, with 10 being high, how confident are you that you can change?"

This is followed by, "What would it take for your confidence to go from a lower number to a higher number?" The answers to the questions will give you insight as to what would motivate the client to change, and you can use that answer to help guide the change process.

Asking Questions That Prompt Clients to Talk About Change

Talking about change can increase confidence in the ability to change. Questions counselors can ask to prompt change talk might include versions of the following:

- "You said you'd like to go back to school to get your GED. What would be a good first step?"
- "What obstacles do you anticipate, and how would you overcome those obstacles?"
- "How would you go about making this change?"
- "What gives you confidence that you can make this change?"

Exploring Real and Hypothetical Sources of Support

Asking a client to talk about his or her connection with someone who has been most supportive and contributed the most to the client's confidence allows him or her to imagine a successful change. Even when a client is resistant—for example, when the answer is something like "My grandfather, and he's dead"—the counselor can invoke hypothetical support like this:

Counselor: "You mentioned that you were afraid to go to the treatment center. Could you pretend your grandfather is with you and providing support when you make this step?"

This technique allows a hesitant client to feel supported as he or she makes this important step.

Reviewing Previous Successes and Personal Strengths

When clients are hesitant or afraid to change, it is often helpful to review other times when they have succeeded and help them examine how they were able to be successful. This may give them confidence that they can make this step as well.

Providing an Escort

The escort accompanies clients to appointments and provides needed support. The escort can be a counselor, a case manager, or a recovery coach. This also creates a feeling of support as the client makes this important step.

As previously mentioned, a major goal of motivational interviewing is to help clients discover their own reasons for discontinuing the harmful behaviors in which they have been engaging. But how does a counselor or therapist know when a client is ready to change? Look for these key transitional moments:

- The client will be less defensive and argue less.
- The client will have better follow-through.

- The client will talk less about the problem and more about the solution.
- The client will begin to ask questions about how to change.

In the end, change must be the client's idea; no one can make a decision for someone else. The counselor's role is a supportive one, and through the use of these motivational interviewing techniques, any counselor will build rapport with clients that can lead to the clients' decisions to change. To help accomplish this, the counselor can do the following:

- Support clients who are ready to change.
- Make sure the plan is the client's plan.
- Stress autonomy of decision making.
- Make sure the client has a variety of options.
- Ask for permission to express any concerns you may have about the plan.
- Summarize the plan.
- Ask the client for a commitment to the plan.

Increasing clients' feelings of urgency to change by helping them see the consequences of not changing, providing a menu of options so that clients have a voice in choosing the pathway of change, and supporting clients every step of the way through that process are all important methods for helping clients take ownership of their recovery and making sure the plan is the client's plan.

eight

Using Motivational Incentives

U SING MOTIVATIONAL INCENTIVES has proven effective with chemically dependent clients (Petry and Martin 2005) and can be used when working with patients who have other issues, including co-occurring disorders, HIV, polysubstance dependence, and criminal behavior. The technique of using motivational incentives is also known as *contingency management,* an evidence-based approach in the treatment of addictions that is derived from one of the basic principles of learning: positive reinforcement increases desired results (Corey 2009). Motivational incentives include any system of rewards (for example, the granting of special privileges, treats, food and clothing vouchers, time off, and so forth) that reinforces positive behavioral change. Motivational incentives are rooted in *operant conditioning*, meaning behaviors that are reinforced are most likely to be repeated. This principle is applicable in many situations and in all walks of life. Some examples of using motivational incentives include:

- **Ice cream (or other treats) for "A" grades on report cards.** Shop owners who participate in this type of incentive report giving out thousands of freebies per year.

- **Computer privileges.** Elementary and middle schools throughout the country report that student behavior often improves when students receive computer privileges for positive behavior.

- **Candy.** A doctor in New York routinely gives candy to heroin addicts at the end of each session. A randomized trial revealed that clients who receive a piece of candy are more likely to come back to the next session (Higgins et al. 2008).

- **Time served for good behavior.** Prisons report that when inmates are given time off for good behavior, negativity in prisons decreases.

- **Reinforcing effects of Alcoholics Anonymous.** Part of the success of Alcoholics Anonymous is the fact that its members receive positive reinforcement every step of the way. They can receive a round of applause for remaining sober for one day, a chip for remaining sober for one month, a medallion for being sober for one year, and a hug for sharing the worst things about themselves in a meeting.

A Brief History of the Use of Motivational Incentives

In the 1960s, B. F. Skinner did groundbreaking research with laboratory rats that proved that positive reinforcement could shape behavior. Skinner and his research associates offered pebbles of food to research rats for pressing a lever. Skinner's theory has been widely used, particularly in education, to reinforce learning among students.

The first widespread use of motivational incentives with chemically dependent clients was in response to the cocaine epidemic that plagued America in the mid-1980s. Researchers wondered if Skinner's principles could be utilized to reward cocaine users for clean urine drops (urine tests). This research involved the use of redeemable vouchers for food, clothing, and toiletries that are awarded for clean urine drops and programmatic retention for cocaine users (Petry and Martin 2005). Programmatic retention can involve staying in the program longer or completing treatment.

In 1986, crack cocaine replaced marijuana as the number-one street drug, and, as it infiltrated urban America, crime increased. The federal government responded by having a war on drugs, including harsh mandatory sentences for conviction of drug use. As often happens, state and municipalities followed the lead of the federal government and offered similarly stringent sentences. Consider that in 1985 there were 400,000 inmates in our nation's prisons. By 1995, the number had swelled to one million inmates, and by 2005, the number reached two million inmates. This increase was in proportion to the increase in individuals with alcohol and drug problems (White, Kurtz, and Sanders 2006). Families were in disarray; the child welfare system got involved, and cocaine-addicted mothers were at risk for having their children placed in the child welfare system if the babies were found to have traces of cocaine in their systems. While all this was occurring, HMOs and managed care were beginning to have a major impact on insurance coverage for chemical dependence. As managed care became the norm, the great majority of inpatient chemical dependence programs across America closed their doors, and the center of chemical dependence shifted from inpatient to outpatient settings (Great Lakes ATTC 2005). This crisis led to the need for new approaches for treating addictions, such as the use of motivational incentives. Over the course of the past twenty years, the use of motivational incentives has been effective with clients who use a variety of drugs and who have a range of other problems (Higgins et al. 2008).

A 2003 research review that examined the effectiveness of redeemable vouchers for cocaine use found that fifteen or sixteen studies revealed a significant increase in cocaine abstinence (Higgins et al. 2003). Studies at Johns Hopkins University found that motivational incentives with cocaine users increased abstinence rates, self-esteem, and self-care, and contributed to family reunification (Higgins et al. 2008; Silverman et al. 1996). Redeemable vouchers for groceries, clothing, personal care items, household supplies, and other items that are important to the client population are more effective in reinforcing for clean drops than cash, because cash is a relapse trigger for many cocaine addicts.

Vouchers have also proven to be effective in increasing programmatic retention. In one study, 85 percent of clients who received vouchers for programmatic participation completed the twelve-week program versus 33 percent of the control group. Redeemable vouchers for clean drops increased sobriety rates as a stand-alone therapy or in combination with other approaches, especially cognitive behavioral therapy. Follow-up studies revealed that the therapeutic benefits of the use of vouchers were sustained after six months. (Higgins et al. 2008).

Principles of Motivational Incentives

When developing motivational incentive programs, a number of principles should be kept in mind.

Choice of Target Behavior

Choose a target behavior that is problematic and in need of change. It is important that the behavior is observable and measurable. Possible behaviors can include group attendance, individual counseling attendance, prosocial behavior, efforts to improve educational, vocational, and occupational capital (enrollment and completion of a GED program, completion of a vocational program, or job readiness program), grades, and abstinence.

Choice of Target Population

Due to economic shortfalls, it may be impossible to offer incentives to every client. Many programs treat chemically dependent women as a priority because of the damage drugs and alcohol have on the unborn, or focus on the criminal justice system because of the staggering associated costs to the society at large.

Choice of Reinforcer

What an adolescent values might be different from what a homeless adult values. When choosing a reinforcer, get input from the target population to help select something a client from that group values and needs. For example, a reinforcer for an adolescent might be a later curfew, computer privileges, or an electronic device, where an adult female with children might be motivated by a food or clothing voucher or a gift certificate for a spa.

Incentive Magnitude

The amount of reinforcement necessary varies among individuals and may be predicated upon the level of past and present drug use, the client's history of success in recovery, or the presence of co-occurring disorders. Recovery capital is also a consideration: unemployed, polysubstance drug addicts will often require higher-level reinforcers than will corporate clients who drink alcohol. In each case, greater reinforcers can often help these clients achieve their goals.

Frequency of Incentives

The frequency with which incentives are offered can be influenced by the resources available as well as the amount of programmatic contact that is desired. The frequency of incentives increases programmatic attendance.

Timing of Incentives

Behaviors are more reinforced when incentives are received immediately after the target behavior.

Duration of the Intervention

Motivational incentives should last at least ninety days for maximum effectiveness; the great majority of chemically dependent clients who relapse do so within the first ninety days of treatment (White 2005). External reinforcers should be discontinued when naturally occurring reinforcers kick in. Examples of natural reinforcers include altruism (client initially attended groups because of motivation to draw from the fishbowl, but, after six months of clean time, is now attending because of a desire to give back to others); gratitude (client has been sober for eight months, is motivated to stay sober, and is grateful for the recovery); and family love (client is now connected to his or her family, trust is increased, and love is returning). The external reinforcers are no longer needed.

Populations That Benefit from
Motivational Incentives

Motivational incentives have proved useful with heroin addicts who are involved in methadone clinics (Higgins et al. 2008). Incentives have included take-home methadone privileges for agreeing to take Antabuse to deter alcohol use, meeting group attendance goals, and the awarding of cash versus take-home methadone. Another effective incentive is the "fishbowl technique," where clients draw chits out of a fishbowl for prizes awarded upon successful completion of targeted behavior. This incentive can increase group attendance as well as increase the number of negative cocaine and heroin urine drops among heroin users. The National Institute on Drug Abuse (NIDA) conducted research on the use of the fishbowl technique, one of the more common approaches used in motivational incentive programs; the findings reveal that the technique is effective in increasing group therapy attendance, decreasing drug use, and improving overall retention rates (Higgins et al. 2008).

Polysubstance dependent clients require a slightly different approach. Research reveals that the use of motivational incentives with this population works best if the client receives reinforcement to discontinue using one drug at a time (Petry and Martin 2002). Combining a reinforcer with a take-home dosage of methadone can be effective with these clients when they are also addicted to heroin (Silverman et al. 2004). Pregnant woman who are chemically dependent have to be encouraged, through the use of incentives, to increase cigarette abstinence, increase clean urine drops, and complete job training programs (Elk et al. 1995; Ker et al. 1996; Donatelle et al. 2000).

Motivational incentives are also effective with adolescents (Wells et al. 2000). Since many adolescents do not believe they have a drug problem and are often resistant to treatment, the use of incentives can be helpful in motivating them to seek help. Incentives can be particularly helpful when parents are involved in determining and distributing the rewards (Petry et al. 2000). Examples of reinforcers for adolescents include awarding allowances and special gifts, increased transportation use and responsibilities, granting later curfews, increasing telephone privileges, and allowing computer and technology use, such as iPods, cell phones, and gaming systems. Behaviors that are particularly important to reinforce with adolescents who have substance use disorders include abstinence, individual and/or group therapy attendance, school attendance, prosocial behavior, grades, and discontinuing nicotine use.

The use of motivational incentives with clients who have co-occurring disorders is helpful, regardless of the psychiatric severity (Sigmon and Higgins 2006). Areas to reinforce include medication compliance, abstinence, therapy attendance, and completion of job-readiness programs. Reinforcers can include cash, special privileges, certificates of completion, housing options, and supportive employment.

Lessons from Drug Court

Drug courts are emerging as an evidence-based approach to addressing addiction and criminality (Higgins et al. 2008). They are specialized criminal courts that provide supervised drug treatment and case management in lieu of prison. The rationale for the use of specialized drug courts in the criminal justice system are the alarming statistics listed below (Belenko and Peugh 1998; Belenko 2001; Langan and Levin 2002):

- Eighty percent of inmates and 67 percent of probationers have a substance use disorder.

- Two-thirds of clients in long-term residential programming have histories of incarceration.

- Fifty percent of clients in outpatient chemical dependency programs have arrest histories.

- Twenty-five percent of clients in methadone maintenance programs are either awaiting a trial, on parole or probation, or mandated to treatment.

- Eighty percent of chemically dependent clients released from prison return to drug use within one year of release. Ninety-five percent return to use within three years. Seventy-five percent are rearrested within three years.

- Seventy percent of probationers and parolees who are referred to chemical dependency treatment drop out.

Why Drug Courts Work

Drug courts are effective because they are consistent with operant conditioning principles and the use of motivational incentives. Drug courts produce twice the abstinence rates as traditional programming for criminal justice clients. Clients involved in drug courts have 60 to 70 percent programmatic completion rates, compared to 30 percent of control groups (Higgins et al. 2008). Drug courts are effective because they offer specific incentives not available in the typical criminal justice system. Consistent with principles of motivational incentives, drug courts are able to offer immediate rewards for desired behavior, such as certificates of completion, reduced sentences, expungement, and immediate sanctions for undesirable behavior. In the traditional criminal justice system, if a client commits a crime or violates probation, there may be months—even years—between arrest and sentence. With drug courts, the judge has the power to authorize immediate sanctions. These sanctions can include written assignments, verbal reprimands, community service, and weekends in prison.

Raising Funds for Motivational Incentives Programs

The success of motivational incentives is backed with research and sounds like it might work for your client or group—yet, it is expensive. There are strategies you can employ to create funding for this type of incentive program. Some of the ways to make it more affordable include staff donations, fund-raising events, and solicitation of local restaurants, grocery stores, and businesses. For example, a colleague of mine utilizes the fishbowl technique to motivate clients who have triple challenges—chemical dependence, HIV, and homelessness—to attend groups. She has had all prizes donated through Walmart, Kmart, and Sears.

Don't underestimate the availability of other philanthropic options available to you: church collections, sponsorship by large and small corporations, and local and national foundations. Advertise your motivational incentives program in the agency newsletter and brainstorm ideas with staff. They have a vested interest in the success of the program, and you might be surprised at their creativity in identifying additional sources of funding.

The use of motivational incentives began as an experiment in the midst of the crack-cocaine epidemic of the mid-1980s. Their use has since proven to be effective over the course of three decades in inpatient and outpatient settings, in urban and rural environments, and with a wide range of client populations, including heroin addicts, polysubstance dependent clients, pregnant women, adolescents, clients with co-occurring disorders, and chemically dependent clients who are in the criminal justice system. Behaviors that are reinforced are most often repeated, and this concept is the basis for the use of motivational incentives to help clients who might otherwise slip through the cracks.

nine

Engaging Clients in Cross-Cultural Counseling

CULTURAL DIFFERENCES between counselor and client can be a major barrier in building rapport, which is a prerequisite in the counseling relationship (Corey 2009). A lack of rapport can increase the chance that clients will miss scheduled appointments, not follow through on referrals, or drop out of treatment prematurely (Duncan, Miller, and Sparks 2004).

Racial and cultural tension that exists in the larger society can also be present in the counseling relationship (Sue and Sue 2007). Clients may view the counselor as "a part of the system," and often this tension has been further exacerbated by disparities in prison sentences based on race (Robinson 2002). Discrimination in employment and housing also may make many clients distrust the counseling relationship (Sue and Sue 2007). When counselor and client are from different cultural groups, the counseling relationship can begin with even more tension and mistrust. This chapter describes seven strategies that cross-cultural counselors can use to build effective rapport with clients from diverse backgrounds.

Build Bridges, Not Walls

The effective counselor employs a multitude of strategies when working with any client; these strategies must be incorporated with additional sensitivity when the client is from a different culture with an eye toward building a bridge of understanding that transcends differences.

Be Aware of Bias

The successful counselor has an awareness of his or her personal biases, assumptions, and stereotypes, and strives to keep them from interfering with the counseling work. To develop this awareness, some counselors utilize journaling exercises with a commitment to honesty. There they describe their biases, assumptions, and stereotypes and how they developed. Other counselors are willing to receive feedback from colleagues concerning ways in which they may be harming clients inadvertently through their biases; they may be blind to these biases, but their colleagues recognize them. Other counselors have made commitments to attend workshops that focus on how to develop cultural competence and eliminate biases and racism.

Increase Credibility

Taking time to increase credibility in the cross-cultural counseling relationship is an effective strategy that reaps continued rewards. Clients often look at more than academic degrees to assess if their helpers are credible (Sue and Sue 1990). Other benchmarks of credibility include:

Sincerity

Since it is difficult to have complete knowledge of another culture, it is possible for a counselor to insult clients inadvertently by saying the wrong thing. Helper sincerity is the one thing that allows clients to forgive helpers who violate a cultural boundary.

Service Energy

When helpers put out a minimal amount of energy, clients often feel that it has something to do with ethnic differences. High service energy increases helper credibility by sending a message to clients that they are valued.

Knowledge of the Client's Culture

Credibility increases as helpers acquire knowledge of the client's culture (Sue and Sue 2007). This knowledge is not gained to "impress the client," but rather to increase empathy in the cross-cultural counseling relationship. For example, if the client speaks

English as a second language, it is often helpful for the counselor to learn key words and phrases from the client's first language. When the client sees the helper struggle to learn the client's first language, this acts as another equalizer.

A Nonjudgmental Attitude

In focus group interviews, this author asked female African American clients to list qualities they found undesirable in helping professionals. Their number-one response was "helpers who judge their romantic relationships." Helping professionals acknowledge a similar bias: focus group participants revealed that they find it extremely difficult to avoid judging the relationship patterns of African American women (Sanders 2001a). One method of overcoming judgments is to treat them as learning experiences. Each time you find yourself judging a client based on cultural differences, you can treat it as an opportunity to learn more about that client's culture. At a 2006 recovery month celebration held in Madison, Wisconsin, a Native American participant stated, "Alcoholism is not a part of Native American culture. It is our response to years of oppression."

Counselor Resourcefulness

Helping clients obtain needed resources such as entitlements, job readiness programs, legal representation, housing, energy assistance, and medical care demonstrates credibility.

Be Sensitive

Clients rarely tell their caseworkers or counselors directly that they are having difficulty working with them because of cultural differences. They often send the message indirectly by talking about past personal experiences (often negative ones) that they have had with members of the counselor's cultural group. This is often a good time for the counselor to explore what it is like for the client to be working with him or her as a counselor. Here are examples of these discussions:

African American client: "I have had a very difficult time working with my white supervisor at work. White police officers often follow me in my neighborhood."

Counselor's response: "You have been talking about your experiences with people who are white. What is it like to be working with me, a white counselor?"

Mexican American client: "Blacks and Mexicans are always fighting in my neighborhood. My son recently got into a fight with a black kid."

Counselor's response: "You sound distraught. On a number of occasions you have mentioned painful interactions that you have had with blacks. What is it like for you to meet with me, a black counselor?"

In most instances, the client will chuckle, laugh uncomfortably, or respond, "I have no problem working with you." While his or her answer may appear vague or avoidant, the interaction almost always increases rapport between the counselor and client, because the client feels that if a counselor is willing to explore issues of race and other differences, he or she must really want to make a connection.

Be Aware of Cultural Tensions

Current and historical tensions can exist between the different cultures of client and counselor. When there is tension in the cross-cultural relationship, there is a lack of trust, which increases the probability of premature termination. The ability to talk openly about the tension removes a barrier to trust. Even if the client refuses to discuss the tension, the fact that the counselor cares enough to mention it can be instrumental in improving the therapeutic relationship. The client thinks, "This counselor must really want to connect with me. I know that cultural differences are difficult to talk about, so she would not bring it up unless she wants to build a relationship."

Take a Student Approach

Allowing the client to be the teacher about his or her cultural experience establishes an egalitarian relationship. Counselors will do a better job of establishing rapport if they take a "curious" rather than an "all-knowing" posture concerning the client's culture. Questions that demonstrate curiosity include: "How have you or your family dealt with this problem in the past?" "Do you have a cultural explanation as to the cause of this problem? If yes, what is the cause?" "How are problems such as this usually dealt with in your culture?"

Be Aware of Ethnic Diversity

Different clients from the same ethnic group should never be lumped into one category. There are religious, socioeconomic, geographical, and educational differences that exist among individuals from the same ethnic group (Sue and Sue 2007). Consider for a moment the numerous cultural differences between poor white clients from Appalachia and wealthy white clients who live in Beverly Hills, California. From a clinical perspective, it is wise to approach a youth from Chicago who is on probation for the distribution of marijuana in a different manner from that used with a Jamaican youth from Brooklyn who says he smokes marijuana as a part of Rastafarian culture.

Incorporate Client's Culture

Incorporating aspects of a client's culture into the change process means giving a nod to the strength of cultural differences that are part of the client's life. This does not necessarily involve a complete overhaul of a program. Subtle steps that counselors can take to ensure that culture is taken into consideration include:

- Asking clients how they view the problems and their views of the solutions to the problems from their cultural perspectives.

- Never viewing clients in isolation, particularly if they come from cultures that traditionally view the extended family as the primary unit (Sue and Sue 2007). Some of these groups include Latinos, African Americans, and Native Americans. Mentioning the client's family during sessions and inviting them into sessions might be quite helpful.

- Referring clients to culturally sensitive service providers. After working with a client, some counselors will make referrals to other professionals to address issues they may not specialize in, and it is helpful to make referrals to other counselors who are culturally sensitive.

- Recommending to clients that they embrace the most healing and supportive aspects of their cultures as a part of their recovery. Many Native Americans in recovery have found that returning to traditions such as the use of the medicine wheel, sweat lodges, and other native traditions have facilitated recovery. Studies of African American women show that many will begin their recovery within a traditional program and maintain that recovery by transitioning into African American, faith-based communities (White, Kurtz, and Sanders 2006).

- Asking bilingual clients if they prefer to attend self-help groups where English or their native language is spoken.

- Encouraging clients to read books, particularly biographies, that tell stories of the trials and triumphs of members of their cultural group.

Connecting with clients cross-culturally and encouraging them to return to the culture that was lost during their active addiction can facilitate recovery. Cohyis and White (2002) outline a 250-year history of various tribes that have successfully incorporated aspects of Native American culture into addictions treatment and recovery. The Nation of Islam has been able to reach African American males who are in the criminal justice system and have been difficult to reach in traditional counseling through the instillation of hope, teaching cultural pride, self-love, and empowerment (McGovern and White 2002).

All counseling is cross-cultural on some level because of the influences of race, culture, religion, education, age, sexual orientation, and other differences between people. It is important for counselors to be aware of these differences and of their own biases concerning them. It is important for the counselor to be alert to his or her clients' level of comfort with differences in the counseling relationship. Counselors must possess a level of comfort in talking about these differences and a willingness and ability to incorporate the client's culture into the change process.

ten

Reassessment of Chronically Relapsing Clients

A CLIENT'S CONTINUAL RELAPSE is often caused by one or more hidden problems. Programs are often funded to focus on one area of specialization, and when other areas are deemphasized, those other problems are not addressed. These hidden problems require careful reevaluation if the client is to move toward recovery. Many mental health workers are not trained in detecting issues of client addiction, many addictions counselors are not trained to detect mental health issues, and very few programs address multiple addictions. What should be obvious is missed, and clients slip through the cracks.

Failure to Assess for Other Addictions

The number one drug of addiction is nicotine. Nicotine kills more people than alcohol and all other drugs—legal and illegal —combined. In addition, clients who smoke cigarettes are three times more likely to return to their drug of choice than are clients who do not smoke cigarettes. Clients who routinely combine drinking and cigarette smoking can be triggered to drink when they smoke cigarettes. In some cases, using illicit drugs such as heroin or cocaine requires the lighting of a match; the smoking of a cigarette also requires the lighting of a match and can trigger cravings for heroin and cocaine use (White 2006a).

Assessing for Process Addictions

Addiction to mood-altering behaviors such as gambling, sex, eating disorders, and Internet use can be strongly linked to substance-use disorders; this is called process addiction. Many chemically dependent clients who stop using drugs substitute their drug use with process addictions and vice versa (Carnes 1994). Clinicians should assess for process addictions with clients who are chronic relapsers.

A counselor cannot look at a client and say, "You look like a compulsive gambler" or "You are probably a sex addict." There are no obvious symptoms when a client has a process addiction, such as one sees with cocaine addiction—like dilated pupils or weight loss.

Counselors should routinely ask questions to screen for process addictions with clients who chronically relapse. If the determination is made that there is indeed a process addiction, there are a number of suggestions counselors can make. They can recommend that the client receive individual therapy for the treatment of that addiction along with continuing to receive support for chemical dependence. The counselor can also refer the client to mutual aid groups, where individuals with the same addiction provide support to each other. For example, a compulsive gambler might be referred to Gamblers Anonymous. Clients assessed as having a sexual addiction may be referred to Sexaholics Anonymous, while clients who are compulsive shoppers can be referred to Debters Anonymous or Overspenders Anonymous. The contact information for numerous mutual aid groups that treat process addictions is included in the resource section of this book.

Each client with a process addiction has his or her own unique relapse triggers, and counselors can monitor for those relapse triggers the same way they monitor relapse triggers for chemical dependence. For sex addicts, triggers might include driving through neighborhoods where they acted out, seeing people they once acted out with, watching pornography on television, sitting on beaches, or resentments—which they can use to justify acting out. Triggers for compulsive gamblers might include running out of money, watching sporting events on television, or listening to others talk about gambling.

Monitoring for Hidden Psychiatric Disorders

Approximately 50 percent of chemically dependent clients have a concurrent mental illness. Often, psychiatric disorders are difficult to detect and may range from phobias, obsessive-compulsive disorders, personality disorders, anxiety disorders, and depression. This difficulty in detection is partly because the use of drugs can mimic many forms of psychiatric disorders, and withdrawal from drug use can mimic symptoms of mental illness. In addition, many professionals working in the addictions field are not routinely trained in assessing co-occurring disorders (SAMHSA TIP 42 2005a).

In an ideal world, all chemical-dependence programs would have a consulting psychiatrist who routinely screens for psychiatric disorders. This is especially important with chronic relapsers. But since not all programs do, alternatives include sending staff to trainings where they learn about the assessment and treatment for co-occurring disorders, encouraging staff to provide services in psychiatric programs to learn about mental illness firsthand, or asking a school of psychiatry to provide residents, supervised by a psychiatrist, to work with your clients.

Recognizing Addictive and Abusive Relationships

Relapse pattern assessment is important to conduct when counseling chronic relapsers. Many clients go from drug use to addictive relationships. This involves using relationships similarly to the way they were using drugs—to escape and avoid problems and feelings. Addictive relationships are characterized by extreme jealousy, enmeshment, smothering, abuse, excessive arguing and breakups, or staying in relationships despite adverse consequences (Sanders 2001b). Domestic violence should also be explored, as there is a strong relationship between domestic violence and substance abuse.

Research reveals that it is particularly difficult for chemically dependent women to leave relationships that involve domestic violence, because active addiction makes it difficult for these women to mobilize themselves (Walker 2009). Research indicates that when women have the financial means, they are more likely to leave abusive relationships (Walker 2009).

Counselors can begin to educate clients about addictive relationships and the tendency to substitute an addiction to a drug with an addiction to a person or a relationship. Some of the characteristics of addictive relationships include obsession, the need for constant excitement, extreme jealousy, enmeshed boundaries, the tendency to abandon friends and loved ones when in a relationship, abuse, and the tendency to stay in the relationship despite adverse consequences (Sanders 2001b).

Counselors can also provide information to clients about the differences between addictive and healthy relationships. Among the characteristics of healthy relationships are: each partner is growing and encouraging the other to grow; each has a separate life outside the relationship; the partners have healthy boundaries; there is minimal jealousy; and there is no abuse. Counselors can also encourage clients to enter all relationships with eyes wide open—that is, encourage them to be aware of the good things that are happening in their relationships in the beginning stages but also to be aware of warning signs that are often present in unhealthy relationships.

Finally, one of the last areas of growth for chemically dependent clients is learning to have healthy relationships. During recovery, clients may enter a number of unhealthy relationships before they break this pattern. It is often helpful for counselors to be supportive of this process and to help clients gain insight into their patterns (Sanders 2001b).

Identifying Enmeshment in a Drug Subculture

Many clients who use socially prohibited drugs—that is, drugs that carry the greatest stigma and legal sanctions, such as crack-cocaine, methamphetamines, and heroin—often find themselves migrating toward "tribes." These are groups who use the same drugs, who provide social support to the user, and who have often been shunned by the rest of society. They often have their own language, rituals, customs, mores, styles of dressing, and other defining characteristics. They include motorcycle gangs who use methamphetamines, street gangs, crack-house associates, bar-drinking groups, rave party attendees who use the drug Ecstasy, and others. These groups can sometimes have a stronger hold on clients than the drugs they are using, and when clients are around the group, they are more likely to use drugs (White 1996)

One sign that clients are addicted to a subculture is that they struggle to stay away from the group. They have incorporated so many aspects of this culture into their way of being that it is difficult to disengage. They may wear the group's traditional style of clothing, use the group's language, or listen to the group's music to the point where, even when they are not around the group, they are still affiliated.

Once a counselor has determined that a client is in a drug subculture, there are a number of measures that can be taken to help clients disengage. One method is to ask socratic questions to help clients gauge the pluses and minuses of their involvement in drug subcultures. Questions can include:

- What were you hoping to get out of your affiliation with this group?
- What have been the benefits of your affiliation with this group?
- Have there been any negative consequences of your affiliation with this group? If yes, what are those consequences?
- Are there ever times when you have felt ambivalent about your affiliation with this group?
- Have any of your relapses been triggered by your affiliation with this group?
- If you were to leave this group, what would you miss?
- What challenges would you face if you discontinued your affiliation with the group?

For clients who are ambivalent about their affiliation with a drug subculture or who have expressed motivation to distance themselves from the group, the counselor can brainstorm with the client what they might put in place of the affiliation with this group. It is often helpful to substitute an addiction drug culture with a culture of recovery, which might include moving into a recovery home, attending a recovery school, or immersing oneself in mutual aid groups of recovery (White, Kurtz, and Sanders 2006).

Offering Recovery Support

Many clients relapse because they lack recovery support in their natural environment. The great majority of those who drop out of 12-step and other mutual-aid programs do so within the first ninety days of leaving treatment (White, Kurtz, and Sanders 2006). Recovery management may offer a solution to this lack of support; for more specific information about recovery management, please see Chapter 6.

By fine-tuning our approach to assessment and providing support to clients in their natural environments, we will help more clients stay on a path toward long-term recovery.

Conclusion

EW THINGS DESTROY a counselor's optimism more than
clients who slip through the cracks. Many counselors
enter the helping professions with idealistic enthusiasm
and a desire to save the world—and then it happens: Over the
course of years, they experience one client after another slipping
through the cracks. Their idealistic enthusiasm turns into pes-
simism, disillusionment, and a lack of hope.

In spite of our training to be objective and not personalize client relapse, many of us occasionally wonder whether we are having an impact. We also recognize the many loopholes between
systems that make slipping through the cracks a strong possibility. Many of us who have provided counseling services for chemically dependent clients over the course of our careers rejoice each
time a client gets sober. Many of us have learned from our for-
mer clients that once they recover, recovery becomes an option
in their families for many generations. As we help clients recover,

we indirectly help their families and friends, whom we may never meet.

My hope is that you, the reader, have gained valuable tools that you can utilize immediately to help clients avoid slipping through the cracks. My final hope is that you will add to the list of strategies and share them with other counselors so that they too can be inspired to keep their clients from slipping through the cracks.

Recommended Reading

THESE BOOKS AND RESEARCH-BASED journal articles are geared toward increasing positive outcomes for clients with addictions and multiple addictions. The publications focus on improving individual, group, family, and counseling skills.

Individual Counseling

Ackerman, S. J., and M. J. Hilsenroth. (2003). A review of therapist characteristics and techniques positively impacting the therapeutic alliance. *Clinical Psychology Review*, 23(1): 1–33.

Babor, T. F. (2003). *Treatment Matching in Alcoholism*. New York: Cambridge University Press.

Bell, A., and S. Rollnick. (1996). Motivational interviewing in practice: A structured approach. In F. Rotgers, D. Keller, and J. Morgenstern (Eds.), *Treating Substance Abuse: Theory and Technique*. New York: Guilford Press, 266–285.

Bishop, F. M. (2001). *Managing Addictions: Cognitive, Emotive, and Behavioral Techniques*. Northvale, NJ: Jason Aronson.

Black, C., H. Paz, and R. R. DeBlassie. (1991). Counseling the Hispanic male adolescent. *Adolescence,* 26: 223–232.

Boren, J. J., L. S. Onken., et al. (2000). *Approaches to Drug Abuse Counseling.* Rockville, MD: National Institute on Drug Abuse.

Broome, K. M., G. W. Joe, et al. (2001). Engagement models for adolescents in DATOS-A. *Journal of Adolescent Research,* 16(6): 608–623.

Carroll, K. M. (1999). Behavioral and cognitive behavioral treatments. In B. S. McCardy and E. E. Epstein (Eds.), *Addictions: A Comprehensive Guidebook.* New York: Oxford University Press, 250–267.

Carroll, K. M., B. Libby, et al. (2001). Motivational interviewing to enhance treatment initiation in substance abusers: An effectiveness study. *American Journal on Addictions,* 10:335–339.

DiClemente, C. C., K. M. Carroll, et al. (2003). A look inside treatment: Therapist effects, the therapeutic alliance, and the process of intentional behavior change. In T. F. Babor (Ed.), *Treatment Matching in Alcoholism.* New York: Cambridge University Press, 166–183.

DiClemente, C. C., D. Schlundt, et al. (2004). Readiness and stages of change in addiction treatment. *American Journal on Addictions,* 13(2): 103–119.

Dodes, L. M., and E. J. Khantzian. (1998). Individual psychodynamic psychotherapy. In R. J. Frances and S. I. Miller (Eds.), *Clinical Textbook of Addictive Disorders.* New York: Guilford Press, 479–495.

Donovan, D. M., K. M. Carroll, et al. (2003). Therapies for matching: Selection, development, implementation, and costs. In T. F. Babor (Ed.), *Treatment Matching in Alcoholism.* New York: Cambridge University Press, 42–61.

Donovan, D. M., and G. A. Marlatt. (1993). Behavioral treatment. In M. Galanter (Ed.), *Recent Developments in Alcoholism, Volume 11: Ten Years of Progress.* New York: Plenum Press, 397–411.

Drake, R. E., K. T. Mueser, et al. (2004). A review of treatments for people with severe mental illnesses and co-occurring substance use disorder. *Psychiatric Rehabilitation Journal,* 27(4): 360–374.

Finnegan, D. G., and E. B. McNally. (2002). *Counseling Lesbian, Gay, Bisexual, and Transgender Substance Abusers: Dual Identities.* New York: Haworth Press.

Galanter, M. (Ed.). (2003). *Recent Developments in Alcoholism, Volume 16: Research on Alcoholism Treatment.* New York: Springer.

Godley, S. H., R. J. Meyers, et al. (2001). *The Adolescent Community Reinforcement Approach for Adolescent Cannabis Users.* Cannabis Youth Treatment

(CYT) Series, Volume 4. DHHS Publication No. (SMA) 01-3489. Rockville, MD: Center for Substance Abuse Treatment, Substance Abuse and Mental Health Services Administration.

Godley, S. H., R. A. Risberg, et al. (2002). *Treatment Manual—Bloomington's Outpatient and Intensive Outpatient Treatment Model.* Bloomington, IL: Chestnut Health Systems. www.chestnut.org/LI/APSS/CSAT/protocols [accessed October 18, 2005].

Goldstein, E. G. (2004). Substance abusers with borderline disorders. In S. L. A. Straussner (Ed.), *Clinical Work with Substance-Abusing Clients* (2nd ed.). New York: Guilford Press, 370–391.

Gordon, K. (1993). The treatment of addictive disorders in a private clinical setting. In S. L. A. Straussner (Ed.), *Clinical Work with Substance Abusing Clients.* New York: Guilford Press, 88–102.

Gurnack, A. M., R. Atkinson, and J. J. Osgood (Eds.). (2002). *Treatment of Alcohol and Drug Abuse in the Elderly.* New York: Springer Publishing.

Heather, N., T. J. Peters, and T. Stockwell (Eds.). (2001). *International Handbook of Dependence and Problems.* New York: John Wiley and Sons.

Kent, C. (1997). Ending with clients: Closure in counseling. In S. Harrison and V. Carver (Eds.), *Alcohol and Drug Problems: A Practical Guide for Counselors* (2nd ed.). Toronto, Canada: Addiction Research Foundation, 203–215.

Levin, J. D. (2004). Counseling and therapy techniques in substance abuse treatment. *Issues in Psychoanalytic Psychology,* 26(2): 145–162.

Marlatt, G. A., K. Barrett, and D. C. Daley. (1999). Relapse prevention. In M. Galanter and H. D. Kleber (Eds.), *Textbook of Substance Abuse Treatment* (2nd ed.). Washington, DC: American Psychiatric Association, 353–366.

Marlatt, G. A., and D. M. Donovan (Eds.). (2005). *Relapse Prevention: Maintenance Strategies in the Treatment of Addictive Behaviors.* New York: Guilford Press.

Martino, S., K. Carroll, et al. (2002). Dual diagnosis motivational interviewing: A modification of motivational interviewing for substance-abusing patients with psychotic disorders. *Journal of Substance Abuse Treatment,* 4(23): 297–308.

McCrady, B. S., and E. E. Epstein (Eds.). (1999). *Addictions: A Comprehensive Guidebook.* New York: Oxford University Press.

Meier, P. S., C. Barrowclough, et al. (2005). The role of the therapeutic alliance in the treatment of substance misuse: A critical review of the literature. *Addiction,* 100(3): 304–316.

Miller, G. (2002). *Incorporating Spirituality in Counseling and Psychotherapy: Theory and Technique.* Hoboken, NJ: John Wiley and Sons.

Miller, W. R., and S. Rollnick. (2002). *Motivational Interviewing: Preparing People to Change Addictive Behavior* (2nd ed.). New York: Guilford Press.

Monti, P. M., R. M. Kadden, et al. (2002). *Treating Alcohol Dependence: A Coping Skills Training Guide* (2nd ed.). New York: Guilford Press.

Mora, J. (1998). The treatment of alcohol dependency among Latinas: A feminist, cultural and community perspective. *Alcoholism Treatment Quarterly*, 16:163–177.

Mueser, K. T., D. L. Noordsy, et al. (2003). *Integrated Treatment of Dual Disorders: A Guide to Effective Practice.* New York: Guilford Press.

Najavits, L. (2002). *Seeking Safety: A Treatment Manual for PTSD and Substance Abuse.* New York: Guilford Press.

O'Connell, D., and E. Beyer (Eds.). (2002). *Managing the Dually Diagnosed Patient: Current Issues and Clinical Approaches* (2nd ed.). New York: Haworth Press.

O'Leary, T. A., and P. M. Monti. (2002). Cognitive-behavioral therapy for alcohol addiction. In S. G. Hofmann and M. C. Tompson (Eds.). *Treating Chronic and Severe Mental Disorders: A Handbook of Empirically Supported Interventions.* New York: Guilford Press, 234–257.

Petry, N. M., I. Petrakis, et al. (2001). Contingency management interventions: From research to practice. *American Journal of Psychiatry*, 30: 276–278.

Platt, J., and S. Husband. (1993). An overview of problem solving and social skills approaches in substance abuse treatment. *Psychotherapy*, 30: 276–278.

Prochaska, J. O., C. C. DiClemente, and J. C. Norcross. (1997). In search of how people change: Applications to addictive behaviors. In G. A. Marlett and G. R. Vandenbos (Eds.), *Addictive Behaviors.* Washington, DC: American Psychological Association, 671–695.

Ramsay, J. R., and C. F. Newman. (2000). Substance abuse. In F. M. Dattilo and A. Freeman (Eds.), *Cognitive-Behavioral Strategies in Crisis Intervention* (2nd ed.). New York: Guilford Press, 126–149.

Rounsaville, B. J., and K. M. Carroll. (1997). Individual psychotherapy. In J. Lowinson, P. Ruiz, et al. (Eds.), *Substance Abuse: A Comprehensive Textbook.* Baltimore: Lippincott Williams and Wilkins, 430–439.

Sabin, C., H. Benally, et al. (n.d.). *Walking in Beauty on the Red Road: A Holistic Cultural Treatment Model for American Indian and Alaska Native Adolescents*

and Families. Bloomington, IL: Chestnut Health Systems. www.chestnut.org/
LI/downloads/Manuals/Shiprock-Walking_In_Beauty_on_the_Red_Road
.pdf [accessed October 18, 2005].

Senior, M., M. Smith, and S. Taylor. (n.d.). *EMPACT-Suicide Prevention Center Teen Substance Abuse Treatment Program Treatment Manual*. Bloomington, IL: Chestnut Health Systems. www.chestnut.org/LI/downloads/Manuals/ EMPACT_manual.pdf [accessed January 23, 2006].

Sheehan, M. F. (1991). Dual diagnosis. *Psychiatric Quarterly,* 62: 107–134.

Siegal, H. A., R. C. Rapp, et al. (1997). The role of case management in retaining clients in substance abuse treatment: An exploratory analysis. *Journal of Drug Issues,* 27: 821–832.

Springer, D. W., C. A. McNeece, et al. (2003). Individual treatment. In D. W. Springer, C. A. McNeece, and E. M. Arnold (Eds.), *Substance Abuse Treatment for Criminal Offenders: An Evidence-Based Guide for Practitioners*. Washington, DC: American Psychological Association.

Summers, R. F., and J. P. Barber. (2003). Therapeutic alliance as a measurable psychotherapy skill. *Academic Psychiatry,* 27(3): 160–165.

Witkiewitz, K., and G. A. Marlatt. (2004). Relapse prevention for alcohol and drug problems: That was Zen, this is Tao. *American Psychologist,* 59(4): 224–235.

Woody, G. E. (2003). Research findings on psychotherapy of addictive disorders. *American Journal on Addictions,* 12(3): S19.

Ziedonis, D., J. Krejci, et al. (2001). Integrated treatment of alcohol, tobacco, and other drug addictions. In J. Kay (Ed.), *Integrated Treatment of Psychiatric Disorders*. Washington, DC: American Psychiatric Association, 79–111.

Zweben, A., and M. F. Fleming. (1999). Brief interventions for alcohol and drug problems. In J. A. Tucker, D. M. Donovan, and G. A. Marlatt (Eds.), *Changing Addictive Behavior: Bridging Clinical and Public Health Strategies*. New York: Guilford Press, 251–282.

Zweben, J. E. (1995). Integrating psychotherapy and 12-step approaches. In A. M. Washton (Ed.), *Psychotherapy and Substance Abuse: A Practitioner's Handbook*. New York: Guilford Press, 124–140.

Group Counseling

Atkinson, R. M. and S. Misra. (2002). Further strategies in the treatment of aging alcoholics. In A. M. Gurnack, R. Atkinson, and N. J. Osgood (Eds.), *Treating Alcohol and Drug Abuse in the Elderly*. New York: Springer Publishing, 131–151.

Battjes, R. J., S. Michael, et al. (2004). Evaluation of a group-based substance abuse treatment program for adolescents. *Journal of Substance Abuse Treatment,* 27(2): 123–134.

Brook, D. W., and H. I. Spitz (Eds.). (2002). *The Group Therapy of Substance Abuse.* New York: Haworth Press.

Daley, D. C., and D. Mercer. (2002). *Drug Counseling for Cocaine Addiction: The Collaborative Cocaine Treatment Study Model.* Therapy Manuals for Drug Addiction, Manual 4. Rockville, MD: National Institute on Drug Abuse.

Finn, A. (2002). Group counseling for people with addictions. In D. Capuzzi and D. R. Gross (Eds.), *Introduction to Group Counseling* (3rd ed.). Denver, CO: Love Publishing Company, 351–376.

Gillaspy, J. A., Jr., A. R. Wright, et al. (2002). Group alliance and cohesion as predictors of drug and alcohol abuse treatment outcomes. *Psychotherapy Research,* 12(2): 213–229.

Greif, G. L. (1996). Ten common errors beginning substance abuse workers make in group treatment. *Journal of Psychoactive Drugs,* 28: 297–299.

Ingersoll. K. S., C. C. Wagner, et al. (2002). *Motivational Groups for Community Substance Abuse Programs.* Richmond, VA: Mid-Atlantic Addiction Technology Transfer Center.

Kauffman, E., M. M. Dore, and L. Nelson-Zlupko. (1995). The role of women's therapy groups in the treatment of chemical dependence. *American Journal of Orthopsychiatry,* 65:355–363.

Kent, C. (1997). Ending with clients: Closure in counseling. In S. Harrison and V. Carver (Eds.), *Alcohol and Drug Problems: A Practical Guide for Counselors* (2nd ed.). Toronto, Canada: Addiction Research Foundation, 203–215.

Khantzian, E .J., S. J. Golden, and W. E. McAuliffe. (1999). Group therapy. In M. Galanter and H. D. Kleber (Eds.), *Textbook of Substance Abuse Treatment* (2nd ed.). Washington, DC: American Psychiatric Association, 367–377.

Kiresuk, T. J., A. Smith, and J. E. Cardillo. (1994). *Goal Attainment Scaling: Applications, Theory, and Measurement.* Mahwah, NJ: Lawrence Erlbaum Associates.

Lawson, G. W., A. W. Lawson, and P. C. Rivers. (1996). Group counseling in the treatment of chemical dependency. In *Essentials of Chemical Dependency Counseling.* Gaithersburg, MD: Aspen Publishers, 141–177.

Litt, M. D., R. M. Kadden, et al. (2003). Coping skills and treatment outcomes in cognitive-behavioral and interactional group therapy for alcoholism. *Journal of Consulting and Clinical Psychology,* 71(1): 118–128.

Matano, R. A., and I. D. Yalom. (1991). Approaches to chemical dependency: Chemical dependency and interactive group therapy—a synthesis. *International Journal of Group Psychotherapy*, 41: 269–293.

McCollum, E. E., T. S. Trepper, et al. (2004). Solution-focused group therapy for substance abuse: Extending competency-based models. *Journal of Family Psychotherapy*, 14(4): 27–42.

McCrady, B. S., and E. E. Epstein (Eds.). (1999). *Addictions: A Comprehensive Guidebook*. New York: Oxford University Press.

Nowinski, J. (1999). Self-help groups for addictions. In B. S. McCrady and E. E. Epstein (Eds.), *Addictions: A Comprehensive Guidebook*. New York: Oxford University Press, 328–346.

———. (2003). Self-help groups. In J. L. Sorensen, R. A. Rawson, et al. (Eds.), *Drug Abuse Treatment Through Collaboration: Practice and Research Partnerships That Work*. Washington, DC: American Psychological Association, 55–70.

Perkinson, R. R. (1997). Group therapy. In *Chemical Dependency Counseling: A Practical Guide*. Thousand Oaks, CA: Sage Publications, 69–87.

Petry, N. M., and F. Simcic Jr. (2002). Recent advances in the dissemination of contingency management techniques: Clinical and research perspectives. *Journal of Substance Abuse Treatment*, 23(2): 81–86.

Platt, J., and S. Husband. (1993). An overview of problem solving and social skills approaches in substance abuse treatment. *Psychotherapy*, 30: 276–278.

Rawson, R. A., J. L. Obert, et al. (1993). Relapse prevention models for substance abuse treatment. *Psychotherapy*, 30: 284–298.

Reilly, P. M., and M. S. Shopshire. (2002). *Anger Management for Substance Abuse and Mental Health Clients: A Cognitive Behavioral Therapy Manual*. Rockville, MD: Center for Substance Abuse Treatment, Substance Abuse and Mental Health Services Administration.

Rugel, R. P. (1991). Addiction treatment in groups: A review of therapeutic factors. *Small Group Research*, 22: 475–491.

Sampl, S., and R. Kadden. (2001). *Motivational Enhancement Therapy and Cognitive Behavioral Therapy for Adolescent Cannabis Users: 5 Sessions*. Cannabis Youth Treatment Series, Volume 1. DHHS Publication No. (SMA) 01-3486. Rockville, MD: Center for Substance Abuse Treatment, Substance Abuse and Mental Health Services Administration.

Schwebel, R. (2004). *The Seven Challenges Manual*. Tucson, AZ: Viva Press. www.sevenchallenges.com/7c_Manual.pdf [accessed November 9, 2005].

Senior, M., M. Smith, and S. Taylor. (n.d.) *EMPACT-Suicide Prevention Center Teen Substance Abuse Treatment Program Treatment Manual.* Bloomington, IL: Chestnut Health Systems. www.chestnut.org/LI/downloads/Manual/EMPACT_manual.pdf [accessed January 23, 2006].

Shaw, S. (1999). Group therapy with adolescents. In G. W. Lawson and A. W. Lawson (Eds.), *Adolescent Substance Abuse: Etiology, Treatment, and Prevention.* Gaithersburg, MD: Aspen Publishers, 121–131.

Springer, D. W., C. A. McNeese, and E. M. Arnold. (2003). Group intervention. In D. W. Springer, C. A. McNeece, and E. M. Arnold (Eds.), *Substance Abuse Treatment for Criminal Offenders: An Evidence-Based Guide for Practitioners.* Washington, DC: American Psychological Association.

Springer, D. W., and S. H. Orsbon. (2002). Families helping Families: Implementing a multifamily therapy group with substance-abusing adolescents. *Health and Social Work,* 27(3): 204–207.

Straussner, S. L. (1997). Group treatment with substance abusing clients. *Health and Social Work,* 27(3): 204–207.

Vannicelli, M. (2002). A dualistic model for group treatment of alcohol problems: Abstinence-based treatment for alcoholics, moderation training for problem drinkers. *International Journal of Group Psychotherapy,* 52(2): 189–213.

Velasquez, M. M. (2001). *Group Treatment for Substance Abuse: A Stages of Change Therapy Manual.* New York: Guilford Press.

Washton, A. M. (1997). Structured outpatient group therapy. In J. H. Lowinson, P. Ruiz, et al. (Eds.), *Substance Abuse: A Comprehensive Textbook* (3rd ed.). Baltimore: Lippincott Williams and Wilkins, 400–448.

Washton, A. M. (2002). Outpatient groups at different stages of substance abuse treatment: Preparation, initial abstinence, and relapse prevention. In D. W. Brook and H. I. Spitz (Eds.), *Group Therapy of Substance Abuse.* New York: Haworth Press, 99–121.

Webb, C., M. Scudder, et al. (2002). *The Motivational Enhancement Therapy and Cognitive Behavioral Therapy Supplement: 7 Sessions of Cognitive Behavioral Therapy for Adolescent Cannabis Users.* Cannabis Youth Treatment Series, Volume 2. DHHS Publication No (SMA) 02-3659. Rockville, MD: Center for Substance Abuse Treatment, Substance Abuse and Mental Health Services Administration.

Counseling Families, Couples, and Significant Others

Black, C., H. Paz, and R. R. DeBlassie. (1991). Counseling the Hispanic male adolescent. *Adolescence,* 26: 223–232.

Brown, A. H., C. E. Grella, and L. Cooper. (2002). Living it or learning it: Attitudes and beliefs about experience and expertise in treatment for the dually diagnosed. *Contemporary Drug Problems,* 29(4): 687–710.

Brown, S. L. (Ed.). (1995). *Treating Alcoholism.* San Francisco: Jossey-Bass.

Brown, S., and V. Lewis. (1999). *The Alcoholic Family in Recovery: A Developmental Model.* New York: Guilford Press.

Cavacuiti, C. A. (2004). You, me, and drugs, a love triangle: Important considerations when both members of a couple are abusing substances. *Substance Use and Misuse,* 39(4): 645–656.

Center for Substance Abuse Treatment. (2004). *Substance Abuse Treatment and Family Therapy.* Treatment improvement Protocol (TIP) Series 39. DHHS Publication No. (SMA) 04-3957. Rockville, MD: Substance Abuse and Mental Health Services Administration.

Chan, J. G. (2003). An examination of family-involved approaches to alcoholism treatment. *Family Journal: Counseling and Therapy for Couples and Families,* 1(2): 129–138.

Cormack, C., and A. Carr. (2000). Drug abuse. In A. Carr (Ed.), *What Works for Children and Adolescents? A Critical Review of Psychological Interventions with Children, Adolescents and Their Families.* London: Routledge, 155–177.

DeCivita, M., P. L. Dobkin, et al. (2000). A study of barriers to the engagement of significant others in adult addiction treatment. *Journal of Substance Abuse Treatment,* 19(2): 135–144.

Epstein, E. E., and B. S. McCrady. (2002). Couple therapy in the treatment of alcohol problems. In A. S. Gurman and N. S. Jacobson (Eds.), *Clinical Handbook of Couple Therapy* (3rd ed.).

Fenton, L. R., J. J. Cecero, et al. (2001). Perspective is everything: The predictive validity working alliance instruments. *Journal of Psychotherapy Practice and Research,* 10(4): 262–268.

Freeman, E. M. (1993). Substance abuse treatment: Continuum of care in service to families. In E. M. Freeman (Ed.), *Substance Abuse Treatment: A Family Systems Perspective.* Newbury Park, CA: Sage Publications, 1–20.

Hamilton, N. L., L. B. Brantley, et al. (2001). *Family Support Network for Adolescent Cannabis Users*. Cannabis Youth Treatment Series, Volume 3. DHHS Publication No. (SMA) 01-3488. Rockville, MD: Center for Substance Abuse Treatment, Substance Abuse.

Joe, G. W., D. D. Simpson, et al. (2001). Relationships between counseling rapport and drug abuse treatment outcomes. *Psychiatric Services,* 52(9): 1223–1229.

Kaughman, E. (1991). The family in drug and alcohol addiction. In N. S. Miller (Ed.), *Comprehensive Handbook of Drug and Alcohol Addiction.* New York: Marcel Dekker, 851–876.

Kinney, J. (2000). Treatment techniques and approaches. In *Loosening the Grip: A Handbook of Alcohol Information* (6th ed.). New York: McGraw-Hill, 558.

Knight, D. K. and D. D. Simpson. (1999). Family assessment. In P. J. Ott, R. E. Tarter, and R. T. Ammerman (Eds.), *Sourcebook on Substance Abuse: Etiology, Assessment, and Treatment.* Boston: Allyn and Bacon, 236–247.

Latimer, W. W., K. C. Winters, et al. (2003). Integrated family and cognitive-behavioral therapy for adolescent substance abusers: A stage I efficacy study. *Drug and Alcohol Dependence,* 71: 303–317.

Lawson, A. W., and G. W. Lawson. (2005). Families and Drugs. In R. H. Coombs (Ed.), *Addiction Counseling Review: Preparing for Comprehensive, Certification and Licensing Examinations.* Mahwah, NJ: Lawrence Erlbaum Associates, 175–199.

Lewis, J. A., R. Q. Dana, and G. A. Blevins. (2001). *Substance Abuse Counseling* (3rd ed.). Pacific Grove, CA: Brooks/Cole.

Lewis, V., M. Allen-Byrd, et al. (2004). Understanding successful family recovery in treatment alcoholism. *Journal of Systemic Therapies,* 23: 39–51.

Liddle, H. A. (2002). *Multidimensional Family Therapy for Adolescent Cannabis Users.* Cannabis Youth Treatment Series, Volume 5. DHHS Publication No. (SMA) 02-3660. Rockville, MD: Center for Substance Abuse Treatment, Substance Abuse and Mental Health Services Administration.

———. (2003). *Multidimensional Family Therapy for Early Adolescent Substance Abuse Treatment Manual.* Bloomington, IL: Chestnut Health Systems. www.chestnut.org/LI/BookStore/Blurbs/Manuals/ATM/ATM108-Miami, html [accessed October 18, 2005].

McCollum, E. E., and T. S. Trepper. (2001). *Family Solutions for Substance Abuse: Clinical and Counseling Approaches.* New York: Haworth Press.

McCrady, B. S., and E. E. Epstein. (1996). Theoretical bases of family approaches to substance abuse treatment. In F. Rotgers, D. S. Keller, and J. Morgenstern (Eds.), *Treating Substance Abuse: Theory and Technique*. New York: Guilford Press, 117–142.

———. (Eds.). (1999). *Addictions: A Comprehensive Guidebook*. New York: Oxford University Press.

McIntyre, J. R. (2004). Family treatment of substance abuse. In S. L. A. Straussner (Ed.), *Clinical Work with Substance-Abusing Clients* (2nd ed.). New York: Guilford Press, 237–263.

McKay, J. R. (1996). Family therapy techniques. In F. Rotgers, D. S. Keller, and J. Morgenstern (Eds.), *Treating Substance Abuse: Theory and Technique*. New York: Guilford Press, 143–173.

Mercado, M. M. (2000). The invisible family: Counseling Asian American substance abusers and their families. *Family Journal: Counseling and Therapy for Couples and Families*, 8(3): 267–272.

Meyers, R. J., T. R. Apodaca, et al. (2002). Evidence-based approaches for the treatment of substance abusers by involving family members. *Family Journal: Counseling and Therapy for Couples and Families*, 10(3): 281–288.

Meyers, R. J., J. E. Smith, and E. J. Miller. (1998). Working through the concerned significant other. In W. R. Miller and N. Heather (Eds.), *Treating Addictive Behaviors* (2nd ed.). New York: Plenum Press, 149–161.

Mora, J. (1998). The treatment of alcohol dependency among Latinas: A feminist, cultural, and community perspective. *Alcoholism Treatment Quarterly*, 16: 163–177.

National Institute on Drug Abuse (NIDA), J. Szapocznik, et al. (2003). *Brief Strategic Family Therapy for Adolescent Drug Abuse*. Therapy Manuals for Drug Addiction, Manual 5. Rockville, MD: NIDA, 87.

O'Farrell, T. J. (Ed.). (1993). *Treating Alcohol Problems: Marital and Family Interventions*. New York: Guilford Press.

O'Farrell, T. J., K. A. Choquette, et al. (1993). Behavioral marital therapy with and without additional couples relapse prevention sessions for alcoholics and their wives. *Journal of Studies on Alcohol*, 54: 652–666.

O'Farrell, T.J., and W. Fals-Stewart. (1999). Treatment models and methods: Family Models. In B. S. McCrady and E. E. Epstein (Eds.), *Addictions: A Comprehensive Guidebook*. New York: Oxford University Press, 287–305.

———. (2000). Behavioral couples therapy for alcoholism and drug abuse. *Behavior Therapist*, 23(3): 49–54, 70.

O'Farrell, T. J., and C. M. Murphy. (2002). Behavioral couples therapy for alcoholism and drug abuse: Encountering the problem of domestic violence. In C. Wekerle and A. M. Wall (Eds.), *Violence and Addiction Equation: Theoretical and Clinical Issues in Substance Abuse and Relationship Violence*. New York: Brunner-Routledge, 293–303.

Petry, N. M., and F. Simcic. (2002). Recent advances in the dissemination of contingency management techniques: Clinical and research perspectives. *Journal of Substance Abuse Treatment*, 23(2): 81–86.

Platt, J., and S. Husband. (1993). An overview of problem solving and social skills approaches in substance abuse treatment. *Psychotherapy*, 30: 276–278.

Rawson, R. A., J. L. Obert, et al. (1993). Relapse prevention models for substance abuse treatment. *Psychotherapy*, 30: 284–298.

Robbins, M. S., K. Bachrach, et al. (2002). Bridging the research gap in adolescent substance abuse treatment: The case of brief strategic family therapy. *Journal of Substance Abuse Treatment*, 23(3): 123–132.

Rotgers, F., D. S. Keller, and J. Morgenstern. (Eds.). (2003). *Treating Substance Abuse: Theory and Technique*. New York: Guilford Press, 117–142.

Rotunda, R. J., L. West, et al. (2004). Enabling behavior in a clinical sample of alcohol-dependent clients and their partners. *Journal of Substance Abuse Treatment*, 26(4): 269–276.

Rowe, C., H. A. Liddle, et al. (2002). Integrative treatment development: Multidimensional family therapy for adolescent substance abuse. In F. W. Kaslow (Ed.), *Comprehensive Handbook of Psychotherapy: Integrative/Eclectic*, Volume 4. New York: John Wiley and Sons, 133–161.

Rowe, C., E. Parker-Sloat, et al. (2003). Family therapy for early adolescent substance abuse. In S. J. Stevens and A. R. Morral (Eds.), *Adolescent Substance Abuse Treatment in the United States: Exemplary Models From a National Evaluation Study*. New York: Haworth Press, 105–132.

Santisteban, D. A., and J. Szapocznik. (1994). Bridging theory, research, and practice to more successfully engage substance abusing youth and their families into therapy. *Journal of Child and Adolescent Substance Abuse*, 3: 9–24.

Sheehan, M. F. (1991). Dual diagnosis. *Psychiatric Quarterly*, 62: 107–134.

Sholevar, G. P., and L. D. Schwoeri. (2003). Alcoholic and substance-abusing families. In G. P. Sholevar (Ed.), *Textbook of Family and Couples Therapy: Clinical Applications*. Washington, DC: American Psychiatric Association, 671–694.

Shulman, L. H., S. R. Shapira, et al. (2000). Outreach developmental services to children of patients in treatment for substance abuse. *American Journal of Public Health*, 90(12): 1930–1933.

Smith, J. E., J. C. Milford, and R. J. Meyers. (2004). CRA and CRAFT: Behavioral approaches to treating substance-abusing individuals. *Behavioral Analyst Today*, 5(4): 391–403.

Stanton, M. (2005). Couples and addiction. In M. Harway (Ed.), *Handbook of Couples Therapy*. New York: John Wiley and Sons, 313–336.

Stanton, M. D., and A. W. Heath. (1997). Family and marital therapy. In J. H. Lowinson, P. Ruiz, et al. (Eds.), *Substance Abuse: A Comprehensive Textbook*. Baltimore: Lippincott Williams and Wilkins, 448–454.

Stellato-Kabat, D., J. Stellato-Kabat, and J. Garrett,. (1995). Treating chemical-dependent couples and families. In A. M. Washton (Ed.), *Psychotherapy and Substance Abuse: A Practitioner's Handbook*. New York: Guilford Press, 314–336.

Szapocznik, J., O. Hervis, et al. (2003). *Brief Strategic Family Therapy for Adolescent Drug Abuse*. Therapy Manuals for Drug Addiction, Manual 5. NIH Publication Number 03-4751. Rockville, MD: National Institute on Drug Abuse.

Szapocznik, J., and R. A. Williams. (2000). Brief strategic family therapy: Twenty-five years of interplay among theory, research, and practice in adolescent behavior problems and drug abuse. *Clinical Child and Family Psychology Review*, 3(2): 117–134.

Thomas, C., and J. Corcoran. (2001). Empirically based marital and family interventions for alcohol abuse: A review. *Research on Social Work Practice*, 11(5): 549–575.

Vaughn, M. G., and M. O. Howard. (2004). Adolescent substance abuse treatment: A synthesis of controlled evaluations. *Research on Social Work Practice*, 14(5): 325–335.

Vedel, E., and P. M. G. Emmelkamp. (2004). Behavioral couple therapy in the treatment of a female alcohol-dependent patient with comorbid depression, anxiety, and personality disorders. *Clinical Case Studies*, 3(3): 187–205.

Velleman, R. (2001). *Counseling for Alcohol Problems* (2nd ed.). Thousand Oaks, CA: Sage Publications.

Velleman, R., and L. Templeton. (2002). Family interventions in substance misuse. In T. Petersen and A. McBride (Eds.), *Working with Substance Misusers*. London, UK: Routledge, Taylor & Francis Group.

Wakefield, P. J., R. E. Williams, et al. (1996). *Couple Therapy for Alcoholism: A Cognitive-Behavioral Treatment Manual.* New York: Guilford Press.

Waldron, H. B., and N. Slesnick. (1998). Treating the family. In W. R. Miller and N. Heather (Eds.), *Treating Addictive Behaviors* (2nd ed.). New York: Plenum Press, 271–283.

Zelvin, E. (1993). Treating the partners of substance abusers. In S. L. Straussner (Ed.), *Clinical Work with Substance-Abusing Clients.* New York: Guildford Press, 196–213.

Resources

National Organizations

Below are the websites of national addictions associations, government agencies, and advocacy organizations.

Addiction Technology Transfer Center (ATTC)
www.nattc.org/
Committed to serving the addictions treatment and recovery services field by staying abreast of what works to enhance their members' skills.

American Academy of Addiction Psychiatry
www.aaap.org/
An international organization of psychiatrists working with addiction faculty at academic institutions, medical students, residents and fellows, and related health professionals to make a contribution to the field of addiction psychiatry.

American Association for the Treatment of Opioid Dependence (AATOD)
www.aatod.org/
Founded to enhance the quality of patient care in treatment programs by promoting the growth and development of comprehensive methadone treatment services throughout the United States.

American Society of Addiction Medicine (ASAM)

www.asam.org

This organization's mission is to increase access to and improve the quality of addiction treatment; to educate physicians, other health care providers, and the public; to support research and prevention; to promote the appropriate role of the physician in the care of patients with addiction; and to establish addiction medicine as a specialty recognized by professional organizations, governments, physicians, purchasers and consumers of healthcare services, and the general public.

Association for Medical Education and Research in Substance Abuse (AMERSA)

www.amersa.org

An organization of healthcare professionals dedicated to improving education in the care of individuals with substance abuse problems.

Center for Substance Abuse Prevention/SAMHSA (CSAP)

www.samhsa.gov/centers/csap/csap.html

Provides national leadership in the federal effort to prevent alcohol, tobacco, and other drug problems.

Center for Substance Abuse Treatment/SAMHSA (CSAT)

www.samhsa.gov/centers/csat/csat.html

Promotes the quality and availability of community-based substance abuse treatment services for individuals and families who need them; works with states and community-based groups to improve and expand existing substance abuse treatment services under the Substance Abuse Prevention and Treatment Block Grant Program; supports SAMHSA's free treatment referral service to link people with the community-based substance abuse services they need.

Children of Alcoholics Foundation

www.coaf.org/

A national nonprofit that provides a range of educational materials and services to help professionals, children, and adults break the cycle of parental substance abuse and reduce the pain and problems that result from parental addiction.

Christopher D. Smithers Foundation, Inc.

www.smithersfoundation.org

Dedicated to educating the public that alcoholism is a respectable, treatable disease from which people can recover while fighting to eliminate the stigma that is associated with the disease of alcoholism.

Drug Enforcement Administration (DEA)

www.justice.gov/dea

Enforces the controlled substances laws and regulations of the United States and brings to the criminal and civil justice system of the United States, or any other component jurisdiction, those organizations and principle members of organizations involved in the growing, manufacturing, or distribution of controlled substances appearing in or destined for illicit traffic in the United States; recommends and supports nonenforcement programs aimed at reducing the availability of illicit controlled substances on the domestic and international markets.

Employee Assistance Professionals Association

www.eapassn.org/public/pages/index.cfm?pageid=1

Promotes the highest standards of employee assistance practice and the continuing development of employee assistance professionals, programs, and services.

Faces and Voices of Recovery

www.facesandvoicesofrecovery.org

Dedicated to organizing and mobilizing the over 20 million Americans in recovery from addiction to alcohol and other drugs as well as their families, friends, and allies into recovery community organizations and networks to promote the right and resources to recover through advocacy, education, and demonstrating the power and proof of long-term recovery.

Harm Reduction Coalition

www.HarmReduction.org

A national advocacy and capacity-building organization that promotes the health and dignity of individuals and communities impacted by drug use.

Johnson Institute

www.johnsoninstitute.org

Promotes the power and possibility of recovery from alcoholism and dependence on other drugs.

Join Together

www.jointogether.org

A collaboration of Boston University School of Public Health and the Partnership at Drugfree.org dedicated to advancing effective drug and alcohol policy, prevention, and treatment.

Joint Commission on Accreditation of Healthcare Organizations (JCAHO)
www.jcaho.org

Sets standards for healthcare organizations and issues accreditation to organizations that meet those standards.

Legal Action Center
www.lac.org

Fights discrimination against people with AIDS, crime records, and histories of addictions.

National Alliance of Methadone Advocates (NAMA)
www.methadone.org

Strives to educate communities and policy makers about the benefits of methadone treatment, support the growth of local advocacy groups, and empower methadone patients with a strong public voice.

National Association of Alcohol and Drug Addiction Professionals (NAADAC)
www.naadac.org

Mission is to lead, unify, and empower addiction-focused professionals to achieve excellence through education, advocacy, knowledge, standards of practice, ethics, professional development, and research.

National Association on Alcohol, Drugs, and Disability (NAADD)
www.naadd.org

Promotes awareness and education about substance abuse among people with coexisting disabilities and enhances access to services, information, and professional helping facilities through the collaborative efforts of interested individuals and organizations nationwide.

National Association of Addiction Treatment Providers (NAATP)
www.naatp.org

Mission is to promote, assist, and enhance the delivery of ethical, effective, research-based treatment for alcoholism and other drug addictions by providing its members and the public with accurate, responsible information and other resources related to the treatment of these diseases, advocating for increased access to and availability of quality treatment for those who suffer from alcoholism and other drug addictions, and working in partnership with other organizations and individuals that share NAATP's mission and goals.

National Association for Children of Alcoholics (NACoA)
www.nacoa.net
Dedicated to eliminating the adverse impact of alcohol and drug use on children and families.

National Association on Drug Abuse Problems (NADAP)
www.nadap.org
Works toward insuring that individuals fulfill their potential by living and working in environments free from substance abuse.

National Association of Drug Court Professionals (NADCP)
www.nadcp.org
Innovative judges, prosecutors, defense attorneys, and clinical professionals created a commonsense approach to improving the justice system by using a combination of judicial monitoring and effective treatment to compel drug-using offenders to change their lives.

National Association of Lesbian and Gay Addiction Professionals (NALGAP)
www.nalgap.org
Confronts all forms of oppression and discrimination practices in the delivery of services to all people and advocates for programs and services that affirm all genders and sexual orientations.

National Association of Social Workers: Alcohol, Tobacco, and Other Drugs Section
www.socialworkers.org/
Works to ensure expanded training of social workers in the substance abuse field.

National Association of State Alcohol and
Drug Abuse Directors, Inc. (NASADAD)
www.nasadad.org
Policies are to strengthen state substance abuse systems and the Office of the Single State Authority (SSA), expand access to prevention and treatment services, implement an outcome and performance measurement data system, ensure clinically appropriate care, and promote effective policies relating to co-occurring populations.

National Black Alcoholism/Addictions Council (NBAC)

www.nbainc.org

A nonprofit organization of people of African American descent committed to educating the public about the prevention of alcohol abuse, alcoholism, and other drugs of abuse, increasing services for alcoholics and their families, providing quality care and treatment, and developing research models specifically designed for blacks.

National Center on Addiction and Substance Abuse at Columbia University (CASA)

www.casacolumbia.org

Brings together all professional disciplines needed to combat abuse of all substances in all sectors of society.

National Clearinghouse for Alcohol and Drug Information

www.health.org

SAMHSA's one-stop resource for information about substance abuse prevention and addiction treatment.

National Council on Alcoholism and Drug Dependence, Inc. (NCADD)

www.ncadd.org

A voluntary health organization dedicated to fighting the nation's primary health problem—alcoholism and drug addiction and the devastating consequences of alcohol and other drugs on individuals, families, and communities.

National Council for Community Behavioral Healthcare (NCCBH)

www.nccbh.org

The unifying voice of America's behavioral health organizations, advocating for public policies that ensure quality care that affords every opportunity for recovery and inclusion in all aspects of community life.

National Institute on Alcohol Abuse and Alcoholism (NIAAA)

www.niaaa.nih.gov

Provides leadership in the national effort to reduce alcohol-related problems by conducting and supporting research in a wide range of scientific areas including genetics, neuroscience, epidemiology, health risks, and benefits of alcohol consumption, prevention, and treatment. Also coordinates and collaborates with other research institutes and federal programs on alcohol-related issues, collaborates with international, national, state, and local institutions, organizations, agencies, and programs engaged in alcohol-related work, and translates and disseminates research findings to healthcare providers, researchers, policy makers, and the public.

National Institute on Drug Abuse (NIDA)

www.nida.hih.gov

Mission is to lead the nation in bringing the power of science to bear on drug abuse and addiction through strategic support and conduct of research across a broad range of disciplines while ensuring the rapid and effective dissemination and use of the results of that research to significantly improve prevention, treatment, and policy as it relates to drug abuse and addiction.

National Organization on Fetal Alcohol Syndrome (NOFAS)

www.nofas.org

Dedicated to eliminating birth defects caused by alcohol consumption during pregnancy and to improving quality of life for affected individuals and families.

Office of Applied Studies (OAS)

www.oas.samhsa.gov

Provides the latest national data on alcohol, tobacco, marijuana, and other drug abuse, drug related emergency department episodes and medical examiner cases, and the nation's substance abuse treatment system.

Office of National Drug Control Policy (ONDCP)

www.whitehousedrugpolicy.gov

Establishes policies, priorities, and goals for the nation's drug control program. To achieve this, ONDCP is charged with producing the National Drug Control Strategy, which directs the nation's antidrug efforts and establishes a program, a budget, and guidelines for cooperation among federal, state, and local entities.

Oxford House

www.oxfordhouse.org

A public supported nonprofit umbrella organization that provides a network of residences offering effective and low-cost methods of recovery.

Partnership for Recovery

www.deviatemedia.com/client_sites/partnership/index.htm

Offers unique treatment products, inspirational workshops for professionals, consumers, and families, and professional consultation services.

Physicians and Lawyers for National Drug Policy (PLNDP)

www.plndp.org

A nonpartisan group of the nation's leading physicians and attorneys, whose goal it is to promote and support public policy and treatment options that are scientifically based, evidence driven, and cost effective.

Research Society on Alcoholism
www.rsoa.org/
Serves as a meeting ground for scientists in the broad areas of alcoholism and alcohol-related problems.

Robert Wood Johnson Foundation
www.rwjf.org
A private foundation dedicated to improving health and healthcare for Americans.

State Associations of Addictions Services
www.saasnet.org/
Works to ensure the availability and accessibility of quality alcohol and drug treatment, prevention, education, and related services throughout the country.

Substance Abuse Librarians and Information Specialists (SALIS)
www.salis.org
International association of individuals and organizations with special interests in the exchange and dissemination of alcohol, tobacco, and other drug information.

Substance Abuse and Mental Health Services Administration (SAMHSA)
www.samhsa.gov
Strives to reduce the impact of substance abuse and mental illness on America's communities, and is directed by Congress to effectively target substance abuse and mental health services to the people most in need and to translate research in these areas more effectively and more rapidly into the general healthcare system.

Therapeutic Communities of America (TCA)
www.tcanet.org/
Provides an array of integrated services including addiction treatment, because of the belief that treatment saves money and lives and that recovery restores families and communities.

Treatment Alternatives for Safer Communities (TASC)
www.nationaltasc.org/
Advocates for people in courts, jails, prisons, and child welfare systems who need treatment for alcohol/drug and mental health problems.

Mutual Aid

In years past, addictions treatment was followed by a referral to Alcoholics Anonymous (AA), in spite of the fact that many clients were unmotivated to attend AA meetings. Resistance occurs when clients feel that they have few choices. Without continuing mutual aid support, many are vulnerable to slipping through the cracks. Below is a list of a wide range of mutual aid resources as well as their addresses, phone numbers, and website addresses.

Advocates for the Integration of Recovery and Methadone, Inc. (AFFIRM)
888-METH 7-86
(888-638-4786) (Toll free)
fchristie@afirmfwc.org

Al-Anon Family Groups
1600 Corporate Landing Parkway
Virginia Beach, VA 23454-5617
888-4ALANON (Toll free) or
757-563-1600
wso@al-anon.org
www.al-anon.alateen.org

Alcoholics Anonymous (AA)
AA General Service Office
P.O. Box 459
Grand Central Station
New York, NY 10163
212-870-3400
www.aa.org

Alcoholics for Christ
1316 N. Campbell Road
Royal Oak, MI 48067
800-441-7877 (Toll free)
al4christ333@sbcglobal.net
www.alcoholicsforchrist.com

Alcoholics Victorious
4501 Troost Street
Kansas City, MO 64110-4127
816-561-0567
www.alcohoicsvictoriouis.org

Because I Love You (BILY)
The Parent & Youth Support Group
P.O. Box 2062
Winnetka, CA 91396-2062
818-884-8242
bily1982@aol.com

Bipolar Dream (Online only)
info@a876590.sites
www.bipolardream.com

Bipolar Significant Others
(Online only)
www.bpso.org

Bipolar World (Online only)
bipolarworld@yahoo.com
www.bipolarworld.net

Buddhist Recovery Network
P.O. Box 4
Maryhurst, OR 97036
paul@buddhistrecovery.org
www.buddhistrecovery.org

The Calix Society
3881 Highland Ave., Suite 201
White Bear Lake, MN 55110
651-773-3117
800-398-0524 (Toll free USA/Canada)
www.calixsociety.org

Celebrate Recovery
info@celebraterecovery.com
www.celebraterecovery.com

Chemically Dependent Anonymous
P.O. Box 423
Severna Park, MD 21146
888-CDA-HOPE (Toll free)
www.cdaweb.org

Co-Anon Family Groups
World Services
P.O. Box 12722
Tucson, AZ 85732-2722

800-898-9985 (Toll free) or
520-513-5028
info@co-anon.org
www.co-anon.org

Cocaine Anonymous (CA)
CA World
3740 Overland Ave., Suite C
Los Angeles, CA 90034
310-559-5833
cawso@ca.org
www.ca.org

Crystal Meth Anonymous
CMA General Services
4470 W. Sunset Blvd., Suite 107
  PMB 555
Los Angeles, CA 90027-6302
Hotline: 213-488-4455
www.crystalmeth.org
Depressed Anonymous (DA)

Depression and Bipolar Support
Alliance (DBSA)
730 N. Franklin Street, Suite 501
Chicago, IL 60610
800-826-3632 (Toll free) or
  312-642-0049
www.dbsalliance.org

Double Trouble in Recovery
P.O. Box 17414
Louisville, KY 40217
502-569-1989
info@depressedanon.com
www.depressedanon.com

Double Trouble in Recovery (DTR)

P.O. Box 245055
Brooklyn, NY 11224
718-373-2684
HV613@aol.com
www.doubletroubleinrecovery.org

Dual Recovery Anonymous (DRA)

Central Office
P.O. Box 8107
Prairie Village, KS 66208
877-883-2332 (Toll free) or
    913-991-2703
draws@draonline.org

Emotions Anonymous (EA)

P.O. Box 4245
St. Paul, MN 55104-0245
651-647-9712
info@emotionsanonymous.org
www.emotionsanonymous.org

Families Anonymous (FA)

P.O. Box 3475
Culver City, CA 90231-3475
800-736-9805
Anonymous.org
www.familiesanonymous.org

Gam-anon Family Groups

Gam-Anon
P.O. Box 157
Whitestone, NY 11357
718-352-1671
info3@gam-anon.org
www.gam-anon.org

Gamblers Anonymous

International Service Office
P.O. Box 17173
Los Angeles, CA 90017
213-386-8789
isomain@gamblersanonymous.org
www.gamblersanonymous.org

**Grief Recovery After a Substance
    Passing (GRASP)**

619-656-8414
mom@jennysjourney.org
www.grasphelp.org

Grow, Inc.

GROW in America
P.O. Box 3667
Champaign, IL 61826
888-741-GROW
www.growinamerica.org

Harm Reduction Network

P.O. Box 498
Prince Street Station
New York, NY 10012
347-678-5671
hams@hamshrn.org
www.hamsnetwork.org

**Heroin Anonymous World
    Services, Inc.**

5555 N. 7th Street, #134-408
Phoenix, AZ 85014
livingfree@heroin-anonymous.org

Jewish Alcoholics, Chemically Dependent Persons and Significant Others (JACS)
120 West 57th St.
New York, NY 10019
212-397-4197
jacs@jacsweb.org
www.jacsweb.org

LifeRing Secular Recovery
LifeRing Service Center
1440 Broadway, Suite 312
Oakland, CA 94612
800-811-4142 (Toll free)
service@lifering.org

Marijuana Anonymous
World Services
P.O. Box 2912
Van Nuys, CA 91404
800-766-6779 (Toll free)
office@marijuana-anonymous.org
www.marijuana-anonymous.org

Methadone Anonymous Support
SUPPORT@MethadoneAnonymous.us
www.methadonesupport.org

Millati Islami
A fellowship of men and women who share experiences, strengths, and hopes while recovering from active addiction to mind- and mood-altering substances.
P.O. Box 2100
Douglasville, GA 30133
info@millatiislami.org
323-872-7264

Moderation Management Network, Inc.
22 West 27th Street, 5th Floor
New York, NY 10001
212-871-0974
mm@moderation.org

Mothers on Methadone
Nenama_mom@yahoo.com
www.methadonesupport.org

Nar-anon Family Groups
Headquarters
22527 Crenshaw Blvd., Suite 200B
800-477-6291 (Toll free) or
　310-534-8188
naranonWSO@gmail.com

Narcotics Anonymous (NA)
World Services
P.O. Box 9999
Van Nuys, CA 91409
818-773-9999
fsmail@na.org
www.na.org

Nicotine Anonymous (NiCa)
World Services
419 Main Street, PMB#370
Huntington Beach, CA 92648
877-879-6422 (Toll free) or
　415-750-0328
info@nicotine-anonymous.org
www.nicotine-anonymous.org

Overcomers Outreach

12828 Acheson Dr.

Whittier, CA 90601

800-310-3001 (Toll free) or 877-
    9Overcome (968-3726) (Toll free)

info@overcomersoutreach.org

Recoveries Anonymous (RA)

RA Universal Services

P.O. Box 1212

East Northport, NY 11731

raus@r-a.org; www.r-a.org

Recovering Couples Anonymous

RCA World Services Organization

P.O. Box 11029

Oakland, CA 94611

877-663-2317 (Toll free) or
    718-794-1456

wso-rca@recoverying-couples.org

www.recoverying-couples.org

Recovery International

105 W. Adams St., Suite 2940

Chicago, IL 60603

866-221-0302 (Toll free)

info@lowselfhelpsystems.org

www.lowselfhelpsystems.org

**Secular Organization for Sobriety/
    Save Our Selves (SOS)**

SOS Clearinghouse

4773 Hollywood Blvd.

Hollywood, CA 90027

sos@cfiwest.org

www.cfiwest.org

Sober 24 (online only)

www.sober24.com

Smart Recovery

7304 Mentor Avenue, Suite F

Mentor, OH 44060

866-951-5357 (Toll free) or
    440-951-5357

www.smartrecovery.org

Women for Sobriety

P.O. Box 618

Quakertown, PA 18951-0618

215-536-8026

www.womenforsobriety.org

**National Addiction Technology Transer
    Center (NATTC) Network**

www.attcnetwork.org

National Addiction Technology Transfer Center (NATTC) Network
www.attcnetwork.org

The purpose of the National Addiction Technology Transfer Center (NATTC) Network is to develop and strengthen the workforce that provides addictions treatment and recovery services to those entering the treatment system. The network consists of fourteen regional centers and a national office, and together they take a unified approach to delivering cutting-edge products, services, and resources to support a powerful workforce—a workforce that has the potential to transform lives. The NATTC Network helps states and organizations within those states implement evidence-based practices in the treatment of addictions. Following is a list of the fourteen regional centers and their website addresses.

Caribbean Basin & Hispanic ATTC
Serving Puerto Rico and U.S. Virgin Islands
www.attcnetwork.org/regcenters/index_centraleast.asp

Central East ATTC
Serving Delaware, District of Columbia, Maryland, and New Jersey
www.attcnetwork.org/regcenters/index_centraleast.asp

Great Lakes ATTC
Serving Illinois, Indiana, Michigan, and Ohio
www.attcnetwork.org/regcenters/index_greatlakes.asp

Gulf Coast ATTC
Serving New Mexico, Texas, and Louisiana
www.attcnetwork.org/regcenters/index_gulfcoast.asp

Mid-America ATTC

Serving Nebraska, Kansas, Oklahoma, Missouri, and Arkansas
www.attcnetwork.org/regcenters/index_midamerica.asp

Mid-Atlantic ATTC

Serving Kentucky, Tennessee, Virginia, and West Virginia
www.attcnetwork.org/regcenters/index_midatlantic.asp

Mountain ATTC

Serving Colorado, Idaho, Montana, Nevada, Utah, and Wyoming
www.attcnetwork.org/regcenters/index_mountainwest.asp

New England ATTC

Serving Connecticut, Massachusetts, Maine, New Hampshire, Rhode Island, and Vermont
www.attcnetwork.org/regcenters/index_newengland.asp

Northeast ATTC

Serving New York and Pennsylvania
www.attcnetwork.org/regcenters/index_northeast.asp

Northwest Frontier ATTC

Serving Alaska, Hawaii, Oregon, Washington, and Pacific Islands
www.attcnetwork.org/regcenters/index_northwestfrontier.asp

Pacific Southwest ATTC

Serving Arizona and California
www.attcnetwork.org/regcenters/index_pacificsouthwest.asp

Prairielands ATTC

Serving Iowa, Minnesota, North Dakota, South Dakota, and Wisconsin
www.attcnetwork.org/regcenters/index_prairielands.asp

Southeast ATTC

Serving Georgia, North Carolina, and South Carolina
www.attcnetwork.org/regcenters/index_southeast.asp

Southern Coast ATTC
Serving Alabama, Florida, and Mississippi
www.attcnetwork.org/regcenters/index_southerncoast.asp

Treatment Improvement Protocol (TIP)

Developed by the Center for Substance Abuse Treatment (CSAT), part of the Substance Abuse and Mental Health Services Administration (SAMHSA) within the U.S. Department of Health and Human Services (DHHS), Treatment Improvement Protocols (TIPs) are best-practice guidelines for the treatment of substance use disorders. CSAT draws on the experience and knowledge of clinical, research, and administrative experts to produce the TIPs, which are distributed to a growing number of facilities and individuals across the country. The audience for the TIPs is expanding beyond public and private treatment facilities as alcohol and other drug disorders are increasingly recognized as a major problem.

CSAT's Knowledge Application Program (KAP) expert panel, a distinguished group of experts on substance use disorders and professionals in such related fields as primary care, mental health, and social services, works with State Alcohol and Drug Abuse directors to generate topics for the TIPs. Topics are based on the field's current needs for information and guidance.

After selecting a topic, CSAT invites staff from pertinent federal agencies and national organizations to a resource panel that recommends specific areas of focus as well as resources that should be considered in developing the content for the TIP. Then recommendations are communicated to a consensus panel composed of experts on the topic who have been nominated by their peers. This panel participates in a series of discussions; the information and recommendations on which they reach consensus form the foundation of the TIP. The members of each consensus panel represent substance abuse treatment programs, hospitals, community health centers, counseling programs, criminal justice and child welfare agencies, and private practitioners. A panel chair (or co-chairs) ensures that the guidelines mirror the results of the group's collaboration.

A large and diverse group of experts closely reviews the draft document. Once the changes recommended by these field reviewers have been incorporated, the TIP is prepared for publication, in print and online. The TIPs can be accessed via the Internet at the URL www.kap.samhsa.gov. The move to electronic media also means that the TIPs can be updated more easily so they continue to provide the field with state-of-the-art information.

While each TIP strives to include an evidence base for the practices it recommends, CSAT recognizes that the field of substance abuse treatment is evolving, and research frequently lags behind the innovations pioneered in the field. A major goal of each TIP is to convey "frontline" information quickly but responsibly. For this reason, recommendations proffered in the TIP are attributed to either panelists' clinical experience or the literature. If research supports a particular approach, citations are provided.

Below is a list of each TIP. They can be ordered at no charge at www.kap.samhsa.gov.

TIP 1   State Methadone Treatment Guidelines—under revision

TIP 2   Pregnant, Substance-Using Women—BKD107

TIP 3   Screening and Assessment of Alcohol- and Other Drug-Abusing Adolescents—Replaced by TIP 31

TIP 4   Guidelines for the Treatment of Alcohol- and Other Drug-Abusing Adolescents—Replaced by TIP 32

TIP 5   Improving Treatment for Drug-Exposed Infants—BKD110

TIP 6   Screening for Infectious Diseases Among Substance Abusers—BKD131

TIP 7   Screening and Assessment for Alcohol and Other Drug Abuse Among Adults in the Criminal Justice System—BKD138

TIP 8   Intensive Outpatient Treatment for Alcohol and Other Drug Abuse—BKD139

TIP 9   Assessment and Treatment of Patients with Coexisting Mental Illness and Alcohol and Other Drug Abuse—BKD134

TIP 10   Assessment and Treatment of Cocaine-Abusing Methadone-Maintained Patients—BKD157

TIP 11   Simple Screening Instruments for Outreach for Alcohol and Other Drug Abuse and Infectious Diseases—BKD143

TIP 12   Combining Substance Abuse Treatment with Intermediate Sanctions for Adults in the Criminal Justice System—BKD144

TIP 13   Role and Current Status of Patient Placement Criteria in the Treatment of Substance Use Disorders—BKD161

TIP 14   Developing State Outcomes Monitoring Systems for Alcohol and Other Drug Abuse Treatment—BKD162

TIP 15   Treatment for HIV-Infected Alcohol and Other Drug Abusers—Replaced by TIP 37

TIP 16   Alcohol and Other Drug Screening of Hospitalized Trauma Patients—BKD164

TIP 17   Planning for Alcohol and Other Drug Abuse Treatment for Adults in the Criminal Justice System—BKD165

TIP 31   Screening and Assessing Adolescents for Substance Use Disorders—BKD306

TIP 32   Treatment of Adolescents with Substance Use Disorders—BKD307

TIP 33   Treatment for Stimulant Use Disorders—BKD289

TIP 34   Brief Interventions and Brief Therapies for Substance Abuse—BKD341

TIP 35   Enhancing Motivation for Change in Substance Abuse Treatment—BKD342

TIP 36   Substance Abuse Treatment for Persons with Child Abuse and Neglect Issues—BKD343

Helping Yourself Heal: A Recovering Woman's Guide to Coping with Childhood Abuse Issues—PHD981

Also available in Spanish:

Ayudando a Sanarse a Si Misma (Helping Yourself Heal: A Recovering Woman's Guide to Coping with Childhood Abuse Issues)—PHD981S

Helping Yourself Heal: A Recovering Man's Guide to Coping with the Effects of Childhood Abuse—PHD1059

TIP 37   Substance Abuse Treatment for Persons with HIV/AIDS—BKD359

Fact Sheet MS676

TIP 38   Integrating Substance Abuse Treatment and Vocational Services—BKD381

TIP 39   Substance Abuse Treatment and Family Therapy—BKD504

TIP 40   Clinical Guidelines for the Use of Buprenorphine in the Treatment of Opioid Addiction—BKD500

TIP 41   Substance Abuse Treatment: Group Therapy—BKD507

TIP 42   Substance Abuse Treatment for Persons with Co-Occurring Disorders—BKD515

Addiction Counselor Licensing and Certification Boards

The purpose of addiction counselor licensing and certification boards is to protect the public safety by ensuring that addictions counselors have the knowledge, skills, and ethical preparation that it takes to prevent and treat addictions. This is accomplished by ensuring that these professionals meet state requirements for certification as addiction professionals. These requirements often include a combination of formal college education, successfully passing a certification exam, and continuing education to maintain that certification, update the counselor's knowledge base, and effectively service an ever-changing client population. Many certification boards sponsor annual conferences for counselors and can provide valuable information to assist in helping to keep clients from slipping through the cracks.

ALABAMA

Alabama Alcohol & Drug Abuse
    Association (AADAA)
P.O. Box 660851
Birmingham, AL 35266-0851
Phone: 205-823-1073
www.aadaa.org

ARIZONA

Arizona Board for Certification of
    Addiction Counselors (ABCAC)
P.O. Box 11467
Phoenix, AZ 85061-1467
Phone: 602-251-8548
www.abcac.net

ARKANSAS

Arkansas Substance Abuse
    Certification Board (ASACB)
UALR Mid South
2801 S. University
Little Rock, AR 72204
Phone: 501-569-3073
www.icrcaoda-arkansas.org

CALIFORNIA

California Certification Board of
    Chemical Dependence Counselors
    (CCBOCDC)
5936 Santa Fe Ave.
Huntington Park, CA 90255

Phone: 323-581-8547
www.californiacertificationboard.org

**California Association of Addiction
 Recovery Resources (CAARR)**
5777 Madison Avenue, Suite 1210
Sacramento, CA 95841-3314
Phone: 916-338-9460
www.caarr.org

**California Association of Alcoholism and
 Drug Abuse Counselors (CAADAC)**
3400 Bradshaw Road, Suite A5
Sacramento, CA 95827
Phone: 916-368-9412
www.caadac.org

COLORADO

**State of Colorado, Colorado Department
 of Regulatory Agencies Division of
 Registrations/Office of Licensing**
1560 Broadway #1350
Denver, CO 80202
Phone: 303-894-7766
www.dora.state.co.us./mental-health

CONNECTICUT

Connecticut Certification Board (CCB)
110 National Drive
Glastonbury, CT 06033
Phone: 860-633-8572
www.ccb-inc.org

DELAWARE

**Delaware Alcohol & Drug Counselor
 Certification Board (DADCCB)**
P.O. Box 4037
Wilmington, DE 19807

Phone: 302-888-2334
www.ceattc.org/de_certification.asp

DISTRICT OF COLUMBIA

**District of Columbia Certification Board
 of Professional Alcohol &
 Drug Counselors (DCCB)**
P.O. Box 3550
Silver Spring, MD 20918
Phone: 301-439-5909
www.dccbpadc.com

FLORIDA

Florida Certification Board (FCB)
1715 Gadsden Street
Tallahassee, FL 32301
Phone: 850-222-6314
www.flcertificationboard.org

GEORGIA

**Alcohol & Drug Abuse Certification
 Board of Georgia (ADACB-Georgia)**
24 Perimeter Park Drive, #108
Chamblee, GA 30338
Phone: 678-547-0111
www.adacb-ga.org

HAWAII

**Hawaii State Department of Health—
 Alcohol & Drug Abuse Division
 (ADAD)**
Kakuhihewa Bldg.
601 Kamokila Blvd., Suite 360
Kapolei, HI 96707
Phone: 808-692-7518
www.state.hi.us/doh/rules/ADMRULES
 .html

IDAHO

Idaho Board of Alcoholism/Drug
  Counselor Certification, Inc.
  (IBADCC)
2419 W. State Street, Suite B
Boise, ID 83702
Phone: 208-345-3072
www.ibadcc.org

ILLINOIS

Illinois Alcohol & Other Drug Abuse
  Professional Certification
  Association (IAODAPCA)
401 E. Sangamon Avenue
Springfield, IL 62702
Phone: 800-272-2632 (in state);
  217-698-8110 (outside the state)
www.iaodapca.org

INDIANA

Indiana Counselors & Drug Abuse
  Certification Board (ICAADA)
1800 N. Meridian Street, Suite 507
Indianapolis, IN 46202
Phone: 317-923-8800
www.icaada.org

IOWA

Iowa Board of Substance Abuse
  Certification (IBSAC)
3850 Merle Hay Road, Suite 303
Des Moines, IA 50310-1324
Phone: 515-334-9024
www.iowabc.org

KENTUCKY

Kentucky Board of Certification of
  Alcohol & Drug Counselors
  (KBCADC)
P.O. Box 1360
Frankfort, KY 40602
Phone: 502-564-3296
www.finance.ky.gov/ourcabinet/caboff/
  OAS/op/adcb/

LOUISIANA

Louisiana Addictive Disorder Regulatory
  Authority (LA-ADRA)
628 North 4th Street
Baton Rouge, LA 70802
Phone: 225-342-8941
www.la-adra.org

MAINE

State Board of Substance Abuse
  Counselors (SBSAC)
Maine Department of Professional and
  Financial Regulation
Office of Licensing and Registration
#35 State House Station
Augusta, ME 04333
Phone: 207-624-8620
www.maineprofessionalreg.org

MARYLAND

Maryland Addictions Professional
  Certification Board (MAPCB)
P.O. Box 245
Sandy Spring, MD 20860-0245
Phone: 866-537-5340
www.mapcb.com

MASSACHUSETTS

Massachusetts Board of Substance
  Abuse Counselor Certification
  (MBSACC)
560 Lincoln Street
Worcester, MA 01605
Phone: 508-842-8707
www.mass.gov/dph/bsas/providers/
  certifications.htm

MICHIGAN

Michigan Certification Board for
  Addiction Professionals (MCBAP)
3474 Alaiedon Parkway, Suite 500
Okemos, MI 48864
Phone: 517-347-0891
www.mcbap.com

MINNESOTA

Minnesota Certification Board (MCB)
P.O. Box 787
Forest Lake, MN 55025
Phone: 763-434-9787
www.mcboard.org

MISSISSIPPI

Mississippi Association of Addiction
  Professionals (MAAP)
P.O. Box 13069
Jackson, MS 39236
Phone: 601-933-4994
www.msaap.net

MISSOURI

Missouri Substance Abuse Counselor
  Certification Board (MSACCB)
P.O. Box 1250
Jefferson City, MO 65102-1250
Phone: 573-751-9211
www.msaccb.com

NEBRASKA

Nebraska Health & Human Services
  Regulation & Licensure
P.O. Box 94986
Lincoln, NE 68509-4986
Phone: 402-479-5580
www.hhs.state.ne.us/reg/regindex.htm

NEW HAMPSHIRE

New Hampshire Board of Licensing
  for Alcohol and Other Drug Abuse
  Professionals
State Office Park South
105 Pleasant Street
Concord, NH 03301
Phone: 603-271-6107
www.nhes.state.nh.us/elmi/licertoccs/
  alcohol.htm

NEW JERSEY

Addiction Professionals Certification
  Board of New Jersey
1200 Tices Lane
East Brunswick, NJ 08816
Phone: 732-390-5900
www.certbd.com
www.state.nj.us/lps/ca/faq/alcfaqsll.htm

NEW MEXICO

NM Counseling & Therapy
   Practice Board
2550 Cerrillos Road
Santa Fe, NM 87505
Phone: 505-476-4610
www.rld.state.nm.us/b%2bc/counseling

NEW YORK

Office of Alcohol & Substance Abuse
   Services (OASAS)
1450 Western Avenue
Albany, NY 12203
Phone: 518-473-3460
www.oasas.state.ny.us/index.cfm

NORTH CAROLINA

North Carolina Substance Abuse
   Professional Certification Board
   (NCSAPCB)
P.O. Box 10126
Raleigh, NC 27605
Phone: 919-833-5743
www.ncsapcb.org

OHIO

Ohio Chemical Dependency
   Professionals Services (OCDP)
37 West Broad Street, Suite 785
Columbus, OH 48215
Phone: 614-387-1110
http://ocdp.ohio.gov

OKLAHOMA

Oklahoma Drug & Alcohol
   Professional Counselor
   Certification Board (ODAPCCB)
9301 South I-35
Moore, OK 73160
www.odapca.org

PENNSYLVANIA

Pennsylvania Certification Board
298 South Progress Ave.
Harrisburg, PA 17109
Phone: 717-540-4455
www.pacertboard.org

PUERTO RICO

Certification Board for Professionals
   in Addiction & Alcoholism
Calle Dresde 469
San Juan, PR 00920
Phone: 787-778-2222
www.attcnetwork.org/getCertified/
   certification.asp?oldID=

RHODE ISLAND

Rhode Island Board for the Certification
   of Chemical Dependency
   Professionals (RIBCCDP)
345 Waterman Ave.
Smithfield, RI 02917
Phone: 401-233-2215
www.ribccdp.com

SOUTH DAKOTA

South Dakota Certification Board
 for Alcohol & Drug Professionals
 (CBADP)
3101 W. 41st Street, Suite 205
Sioux Falls, SD 57105
Phone: 605-332-2645
www.state.sd.us/DHS/Boards/CBADP/
 Index.htm

TEXAS

Texas Certification Board of Addiction
 Professionals (TCBAP)
1005 Congress Ave., Suite 460
Austin, TX 78701
Phone: 512-708-0629
www.tcbap.org

UTAH

Division of Occupational &
 Professional Licensing
P.O. Box 146741
Salt Lake City, UT 84114-6741
Phone: 801-530-6628
www.dopl.utah.gov/licensing/substance
 _abuse_counselor.html

VERMONT

Vermont Alcohol & Drug Abuse
 Certification Board
P.O. Box 135
St. Albans, VT 05478
Phone: 802-878-7776
www.vtcertificatonboard.org

VIRGINIA

Substance Abuse Certification Alliance
 of Virginia (SACAVA)
1108 Westbriar Drive, Suite D
Richmond, VA 23238
Phone: 804-741-2319
www.sacava.org

WEST VIRGINIA

West Virginia Certification Board
 for Addiction & Prevention
 Professionals
122 Third Avenue
S. Charleston, WV 25303
Phone: 304-746-2942
www.wvcbapp.org

WISCONSIN

Wisconsin Certification Board (WCB)
734 N. 4th Street, 1st Floor
Milwaukee, WI 53203
Phone: 414-774-7729
www.wisconsincertificationboard.org

References

About the Federal Bureau of Prisons. July 2001. Federal Prison Industries, U.S. Penitentiary, Lompoc, CA. http://www.oplgov/ipapg/ipaabout.pdf.

American Psychiatric Association. 2000. *Diagnostic and Statistical Manual of Mental Disorders, Vol. IV-TR.* 4th Edition.

Beattie, M. 1987. *Codependent No More.* Center City, MN: Hazelden.

Belenko, S. 2001. *Research on Drug Courts: A Critical Review: 2001 Update.* New York, NY: National Center on Addiction and Substance Abuse at Columbia University.

Belenko, S., and J. Peugh. 1998. *Behind Bars: Substance Abuse in America's Prison Population.* New York, NY: National Center on Addiction and Substance Abuse at Columbia University.

Black, D. 1999. *Bad Boys, Bad Men.* New York, NY: Oxford University Press.

Blocker, J., D. Fahey, and I. Tyrrell. 2003. *Alcohol Temperance in Modern History.* Santa Barbara, CA: ABC-CLIO.

Bradshaw, J. 1988. *The Family.* Deerfield Beach, FL: Health Communications, Inc.

Brecht, M. L., L. Greenwell, and M. D. Anglin. 2005. "Methamphetamine Treatment: Trends and Predictors of Retention and Completion in a Large State Treatment System (1992–2002)." *Journal of Substance Abuse Treatment* 29(4): 295–306.

Brown, S., V. Lewis, and A. Liotta. 2000. *The Family Recovery Guide*. Oakland, CA: New Harbinger Publications, Inc.

Buckmin, E. S., ed. 1994. *The Handbook of Humor: Clinical Applications in Psychotherapy*. Melbourne, Florida: Krieger Publishing Company.

California Department of Drug and Alcohol Programs. 2007. *Methamphetamine Treatment: A Practitioner's Reference*. Sacramento, CA.

Carnes, P. 1994. *A Gentle Path Through the 12 Steps: The Classic Guide for All People in the Process of Recovery*. Center City, MN: Hazelden.

Cohyis, D., and W. White. 2002. "Addiction and Recovery in Native America: Lost History, Enduring Lessons." *Counselor*, 5: 16–20.

Corey, G. 2000. *Theory and Practice of Counseling and Psychotherapy*. 6th Edition. Pacific Grove, CA: BrookCole.

———. 2009. *Theory and Practice of Counseling and Psychotherapy*. 8th Edition. Pacific Grove, CA: BrookCole.

Diamond, M. 2009. "Innovation and Diffusion of Technology: A Human Process." *Consulting Psychology: Practice and Research* 48(4): 221–229.

DiClemente, C. 2007. *Addiction and Change*. New York, NY: Guilford Press.

Donatelle, R., S. Prows, D. Champeau, and D. Hudson. 2000. "Randomized Control Trial Using Social Support and Financial Incentives for High Risk Pregnant Smokers: Significant Other Supporter Program." *Tobacco Control* 9: 67–69.

Duncan, B. 2005. *What's Right with You? Debunking Dysfunction and Change in Your Life*. Deerfield Beach, FL: Health Communications, Inc.

Duncan, B., S. Miller, and J. Sparks. 2004. *The Heroic Client: A Revolutionary Way to Improve Effectiveness Through Client-Directed Outcome-Informed Therapy*. San Francisco, CA: Jossey-Bass, Inc.

Duncan, B., S. Miller, B. Wampold, and M. Hubble. 2009. *The Heart and Soul of Change*. 2nd Edition. Washington, DC: American Psychological Association.

Ekleberry, S. 2009. *Integrated Treatment for Co-Occurring Disorders*. New York, NY: Routledge.

Elk, R., J. Schmitz, R. Spiga, H. Rhoades, R. Andres, and J. Grabowski. 1994. "Cessation of Cocaine Use During Pregnancy: A Preliminary Comparison." *Addictive Behaviors* 19: 697–702.

Emmelkamp, P. M., G. and E. Vedel. 2006. *Evidence-Based Treatment for Alcohol and Drug Abuse*. New York, NY: Routledge.

Friedman, M. J., T. Keane, and P. A. Resick. 2007. *Handbook of PTSD: Science and Practice.* New York, NY: Guilford Press

Garbarino, J. 1999. *Lost Boys: Why Our Sons Turn Violent and How We Can Save Them.* Mankato, MN: Free Press.

GLATTC Bulletin. September 2005. Chicago, IL: Great Lakes Addiction Technology Transfer Center. http://www.glattc.org.

Goble, F. 2004. *The Third Force: The Psychology of Abraham Maslow.* Chapel Hill, NC: Maurice Bassett.

Gonzales, R., P. Marinelli-Casey, S. Shoptaw, A. Ang, and R. A. Rawson. 2006. "Hepatitis C Virus among Methamphetamine-Dependent Individuals in Outpatient Treatment." *Journal of Substance Abuse Treatment* 31: 195–202.

Great Lakes ATTC, 2005.

Hermann, J. 1997. *Trauma and Recovery.* New York, NY: Basic Books.

Higgins, S., A. Budney, W. Bickel, J. Hughes, F. Foerg, and G. Badger. 2003. "Achieving Cocaine Abstinence with a Behavioral Approach." *American Journal of Psychiatry* 150(9): 763–769.

Higgins, S., A. Budney, F. Foerg, R. Donham, and G. Badger. 2007. "Incentives Improve Outcomes in Outpatient of Cocaine Dependence Behavioral Treatment." *Archives of General Psychiatry* 51(7): 568–576.

Higgins, S., D. Delaney, A. Budney, W. Bickel, J. R. Hughes, F. Foerg, and J. W. Fenwick. 1991. "A Behavioral Approach to Achieving Initial Cocaine Abstinence. *American Journal of Psychiatry* 148(9): 1218–1224.

Higgins, S., K. Silverman, G. Heil, and J. Brady, eds. 2008. *Contingency Management in Substance Abuse Treatment.* New York, NY: Guilford Press.

Hoffman, D. B., and R. J. Lefkowitz. 1993. "Catecholamines and Sympathomimetic Drugs."*Pharmacological Basis of Therapeutics.* 8th Edition. New York: McGraw-Hill, 187–220.

Holton, W. C. 2001. "Unlawful Lab Leftovers."*Environmental Health Perspectives* 109(12): A576.

Hubble, M., B. Duncan, L. Barry, S. Miller, eds. 1999. *The Heart and Soul of Change: What Works in Therapy.* Washington, D.C.: American Psychological Association.

Ker, M., S. Leischow, I. Markowitz, and E. Merikle. 1996. "Involuntary Smoking Cessation: A Treatment Option. *Journal of Psychoactive Drugs* 28: 47–60.

Kolf, J. C. 1999. *How I Can Help: How to Support Someone Who Is Grieving.* Tucson, AZ: Fisher Books.

Kübler-Ross, E. 1969. *On Death and Dying.* New York, NY: Simon and Schuster.

Langan, P., and D. Levin. 2002. "Recidivism of Prisoners Released in 1994." Bureau of Justice Statistics, U.S. Department of Justice. Washington, D.C.

Larsen, E. 1985. *Stage II Recovery: Life Beyond Addiction.* San Francisco, CA: HarperOne.

Leach, M., and J. Aten. 2010. *Culture and the Therapeutic Process: A Guide for Mental Health Professionals.* New York, NY: Routledge.

Liddle, H., and S. Rowe, eds. 2005. *Adolescent Substance Abuse: Research and Clinical Perspectives.* Cambridge, NY: Cambridge University Press.

Mayeda, S., and M. Sanders. 2007. "Counseling Difficult-to-Reach Chemically Dependent Adolescent Males: A Strength-Based Approach." *Counselor* 8: 32–36.

Maslow, A. Quotation from http://www.quotegarden.com/perspective.html.

McGovern, T., and W. White. 2002. *Alcohol Problems in the United States: 20 Years of Treatment Perspectives.* Binghamton, NY: Haworth Press.

Midwest Recovery Management Symposium for Policy Makers (2005). Great Lakes Addiction Technology Transfer Center. Chicago, IL.

Miller, W., and S. Rollnick. 1990. *Motivational Interviewing.* New York: Guilford Press.

———. 2002. *Motivational Interviewing, 2nd Edition.* New York: Guilford Press

Miller, P. 2009. *Evidence-Based Addiction Treatment.* New York, NY: Elsevier, Inc.

Minkoff, K., and C. Cline. 2004. "Welcoming Systems for Individuals with Co-Occurring Disorders: The Role of the Comprehensive Continuous Integrated System of Care Model." *Journal of Dual Diagnosis* 1: 63–89.

Muesser, K., D. Noordsy, R. Drake, and S. Fox. 2003. *Integrated Treatment for Dual Disorders.* New York, NY: Guilford Press.

National Mental Health Information Center (2004). www.SAMHSA.gov.

National Summit on Recovery. 2005. Conference Report, SAMHSA, Washington, D.C. www.partnersforrecovery.samhsa.gov/docs/summit_rpt_1.pdf.

Nowinski, Joseph, and Stuart Baker. 1992. *The Twelve-Step Facilitation Handbook: A Systematic Approach to Recovery from Substance Dependence.* Center City, MN. Hazelden.

Nowinski, J., S. Baker, and K. M. Carroll. 1994. *Twelve Step Facilitation Therapy Manual: A Clinical Research Guide for Therapists Treating Individuals with Alcohol Abuse and Dependence.* Project MATCH Monograph Series, Vol. 1. DHHS Publication No. 94–3722, Rockville, MD: NIAAA.

O'Connell, D. F., and E. P. Beyer. 2002. *Managing the Dually Diagnosed Patient: Current Issues and Clinical Approaches.* Binghamton, NY: Haworth Press.

Olbert, J. L., M. J. McCann, P. Marinelli-Casey, A. Weiner, S. Minsky, P. Brethen, and R. Rawson. 2000. "The Matrix Model of Outpatient Stimulant Abuse Treatment: History and Description." *Journal of Psychoactive Drugs* 32(2): 157–164.

Petry, N. 2002. "Low Cost Contingency Management for Treating Cocaine- and Opiate-Abusing Methadone Patients." *Journal of Consulting and Clinical Psychology* 70(2): 398–404.

Petry, N., and M. Bohn. 2003. "Fishbowls and Candy Bars: Using Low-cost Incentives to Increase Treatment Retention." *Science and Practice Perspectives* 2(1): 55–61.

Petry, N. and B. Martin. 2005. "Prize Reinforcement Contingency Management for Cocaine Dependence: Integration with Group Therapy in a Methadone Clinic." *Journal of Consulting and Clinical Psychology* 73(2): 354–359.

Petry, N., B. Martin, J. Cooney, and H. Kranzler. 2000. "Give Them Prizes and They Will Come: Contingency Management for Treatment of Alcohol Dependence. "*Journal of Consulting and Clinical Psychology* 68: 250–257.

Real, T. 1997. *I Don't Want to Talk About It: Overcoming the Secret Legacy of Male Depression.* New York, NY: Fireside Press.

Remboldt, C., and R. Zimmerman. 1998. *Respect and Protect.* Center City, MN: Hazelden.

Riggs, P. D., and D. R. Davies. 2002. "A Clinical Approach to Integrating Treatment for Adolescent Depression and Substance Abuse." *American Academy of Child and Adolescent Psychiatry* (41): 1253–1255

Robinson, R. 2002. *The Reckoning.* New York, NY: Penguin.

Rollnick, S., W. Miller, and C. Butler. 2008. *Motivational Interviewing in Health Care.* New York, NY: Guilford Press.

Rosengren, D. B. 2009. *Building Motivational Interviewing Skills: A Practitioner Workbook (Applications of Motivational Interviewing).* New York, NY: Guilford Press.

Rotgers, F., and M. Maniacci. 2006. *Antisocial Personality Disorder: A Practitioner's Guide to Comparative Treatments*. New York, NY: Springer.

SAMHSA. 2009a. TEDS 2007 Highlights Report. http://oas.samhsa.gov/TED S2k7highlights/TOC.cfm.

SAMHSA TIP 42. 2005a. Substance Abuse Treatment for Persons with Co-Occurring Disorders. Rockville, MD: U.S. Department of Health and Human Services.

SAMHSA TIP 44. 2005b. Substance Abuse Treatment for Adults in the Criminal Justice System. Rockville, MD: U.S. Department of Health and Human Services.

SAMHSA TIP 35. 2008. Enhancing Motivation for Change in Substance Abuse Treatment. Rockville, MD: U.S. Department of Health and Human Services.

SAMHSA TIP 52. 2009b. Clinical Supervision and Professional Development of the Substance Abuse Counselor. Rockville, MD: U.S. Department of Health and Human Services.

Sanders, M. 1993. *Treating the African American Male Substance Abuser*. Chicago: Winds of Change.

———. 2001a. *Counseling Chemically Dependent African American Women*. Chicago, IL: Winds of Change.

———. 2001b. *Relationship Detox: How to Have Healthy Relationshipsin Recovery*. Chicago: Winds of Change.

———. 2002a. "Blending Grief Therapy and Addiction Treatment." *Counselor* 3(6): 40–44.

———. 2002b. "The Response of African American Communities to Addiction." *In Alcohol Problems in the United States: 20 Years of Treatment Perspectives*. New York, NY: Hawthorne Press.

———. 2003a. *Addiction Counselor Certification Exam Study Course*. Chicago, IL: Winds of Change.

———. 2003b. *Good Grief: Helping Adolescents Cope with Loss*. CD-ROM. Springfield,IL: AATP.

———. 2004. *Helping Chemically Dependent Clients Cope with Loss*. DVD. Springfield, IL: AATP.

———. 2005. *The Therapeutic Benefits of Humor: A Workshop for Professionals Who Work with Difficult-to-Reach Adolescents*. CD-ROM. Deerfield Beach, FL: Adolescent Services, Health Communications Services, Inc.

————. 2008. "Recovery Management and People of Color." *Alcoholism Treatment Quarterly.* 26(3): 365-395.

————. 2009. "Recovery Management with Methamphetamine Addicts in Rural America" [Electronic version]. Retrieved from SAMHSA E-Network at: www. onthemarkconsulting25.com/Documents/Recovery%20Management%20 With%20Methamphetamine%20Addicts%20In%20Rural%20America.pdf.

Sharry, J. 2004. *Counseling Children, Adolescents, and Families: A Strength-Based Approach.* Thousand Oaks, CA: Sage Publications, Inc.

Sigmon, S., and S. Higgins. 2006. "Voucher-Based Contingent Reinforcement of Marijuana Abstinence Among Individuals with Serious Mental Illness." *Journal of Substance Abuse Treatment* 30(4): 291–295.

Silverman, K., E. Robles, T. Mudric, G. Bigelow, and M. Spitzer. 2004. "A Randomized Trial of Long-Term Reinforcement of Cocaine Abstinence in Methadone Maintained Patients Who Inject Drugs." *Journal of Consulting and Clinical Psychology* 72(5): 839–854.

Silverman, K., C. Wong, S. Higgins, R. Brooner, I. Montoya, E. Cone, et al. 1996. "Increasing Opiate Abstinence through Voucher-Based Reinforcement Therapy." *Drug and Alcohol Dependence* 41(2): 157–165.

Sim, T., S. L. Simon, C. Domier, K. Richardson, R. A. Rawson, and W. Ling. 2002. "Cognitive Deficits Among Methamphetamine Users with Attention Deficit Hyperactivity Symptomatology." *Journal of Addiction Disorders* 21: 75–89.

Straussner, S., and S. Brown. 2002. *The Handbook of Addiction Treatment for Women: Theory and Practice.* San Francisco, CA: Jossey-Bass.

Substance Abuse and Mental Health Services Administration, Office of Applied Studies. *Treatment Episode Data Set (TEDS) Highlight--2007 National Admissions to Substance Abuse Treatment Services.* OAS Series #S-45, HHS Publication No. (SMA) 09-4360, Rockville, MD, 2009. Available online at: http:// www.oas.samhsa.gov/teds2k7highlights/toc.cfm.

Sue, D. W., and D. Sue. 1990. *Counseling the Culturally Different.* New York, NY: Wiley and Sons.

————. 2007. *Counseling the Culturally Diverse.* 5th Ed. New York, NY: Wiley and Sons.

Valesquez, M., G. Maurer, C. Crouch, and C. DiClemente. 2001. *Group Treatment for Substance Abuse: A Stages-of-Change Therapy Manual.* New York, NY: Guilford Press.

Walker, L. E. A. 2009. *The Battered Woman Syndrome.* 3rd Ed. (Springer Series Focus on Women). New York, NY: Springer Publishing.

Wells, K., J. Epstein, S. Hinshaw, C. Conners, J. Klaric, and H. Abikoff. 2000. "Parenting and Family Stress Treatment Outcomes in Attention Deficit, Hyperactive Activity Disorder: An Empirical Analysis in the MTA Study." *Journal of Abnormal Child Psychology* 28:543–553.

White, W. 1996. *Pathways from the Culture of Addiction to the Culture of Recovery: A Travel Guide for Addiction Professionals.* Center City, MN: Hazelden.

———. 2005. "Recovery Management: What If We Really Believed That Addiction Was a Chronic Disorder?" GLATTC Bulletin. Chicago, IL: www.Attcnetwork .org/learn /topics/rosc/resources.asp.

———. 2006a. *Alcohol, Tobacco, and Other Use by Addictions Professionals: Historical Reflections and Suggested Guidelines.* Bloomington, IL: Chestnut Health Systems.

———. 2006b. *Sponsor, Recovery Coach Addiction Counselor: The Importance of Role Clarity and Role Integrity.* Philadelphia, PA: Philadelphia Department of Behavioral Health and Mental Retardation Services.

———. 2007. "An Interview with Phillip Valentine." *Perspectives on Systems Transformation: How Visionary Leaders Are Shifting Addictions Treatment Toward a Recovery-Oriented System of Care.* Chicago, IL: Great Lakes Addiction Technology Transfer Center. http://www.attcnetwork.org/learn/topics/rosc/docs/phillipvalentineinterview.pdf.

———. 2008. *Perspectives on Systems Transformations.* Chicago, IL: Great Lakes Addiction Technology Transfer Center.

———. 2009. *Peer-Based Addiction Recovery Support: History, Theory, Practice, and Scientific Evaluation.* Chicago, IL: Great Lakes Addiction Technology Transfer Center.

White, W., and W. Cloud. 2008. "Recovery Capital: A Primer for Addictions Professionals." *Counselor* 9(5): 22-27.

White, W., E. Kurtz, and M. Sanders. 2005. *Recovery Management.* Chicago, IL: Great Lakes Addiction Technology Transfer Center.

———. 2006. *Recovery Management.* Chicago, IL: Great Lakes Addiction Technology Transfer Center.

White, W. L., and A. T. McLellan. (2008). Addiction As a Chronic Disease: Key Messages for Clients, Families, and Referral Sources. *Counselor,* 9(3), 24-33.

White, W., and W. Miller. 2007. "The Use of Confrontation in Addictions Treatment: History, Science, and Time for Change." *Counselor* 8(4): 12–30.

Index

employment, grief and, 74–75
empowerment, therapeutic relationship and, 58–59
energy, credibility and, 133
engagement
    antisocial personality disorder and, 40
    challenges of, 7–12
    strategies for, 12–28
entitlement, antisocial personality disorder and, 40, 42
environment
    recovery approaches and, 36
    recovery management and, 86
    for recovery support, 50
escorts, change and, 116–17
examinations, motivational interviewing and, 105
experience, prior. *See* prior experiences

F
faith-based organizations, partnering and, 34
family
    antisocial personality disorder and, 46
    safety and, 63
    support of, 35
feedback
    motivational interviewing and, 109
    as strategy for engagement, 22
flashbacks, post-traumatic stress disorder and, 66
freedom, law of, 110
frequency, incentives and, 125
friends
    grief and, 75–76, 79
    support of, 35
funding considerations, incentives and, 129–30

G
gambling, 142–43
gang members, trauma and, 54
gender considerations
    challenges to engagement and, 10–11
    recovery coaching and, 96
    sensitivity and, 22
genetics, antisocial personality disorder and, 45
grief
    addiction and, 69–70
    as challenge to engagement, 10
    common losses and, 70–76
    creating memories for loss and, 79–80
    stages of, 76
    strategies for assisting with, 76–79
    termination of therapy and, 81–83
    therapeutic relationship and, 62

group work, grief and, 80
growth, recovery approaches and, 37
guilt, therapeutic relationship and, 62

H
hazing, trauma and, 54
hearing, as trigger, 67
hepatitis, methamphetamine use and, 91
hospitality, as strategy for engagement, 13–14
housing, grief and, 75
humor, as strategy for engagement, 24–27

I
"I heard what I said," law of, 111
impulsivity, antisocial personality disorder and, 41
incarceration
    alternating with crime, 39–40
    antisocial personality disorder and, 41
    trauma and, 54
    vs. treatment, 32
incentives
    efficacy of, 119–20
    funding for, 129–30
    history of, 121–23
    lessons from drug court, 128–29
    principles of, 123–25
indigenous healers, recovery approaches and, 36
individualization, recovery approaches and, 36
initial contact, warmth at, 12–13
instability, antisocial personality disorder and, 44
insurance reimbursement, 32
intake, questions during, 14–15
Internet use addiction, 142–43
interventions
    pacing of, 20
    stage-based, 17–18
interviewing techniques. *See* motivational interviewing
in-treatment support, 88–89
investment, self-determination and, 35
irresponsibility, antisocial personality disorder and, 42
irritability, antisocial personality disorder and, 41
isolation, methamphetamine use and, 92

J
journaling, grief and, 80
judgment, credibility and, 134
Jung, Carl, 29
justification, antisocial personality disorder and, 42

About the Author

Mark Sanders, LCSW, CADC, is a member of the faculty of the Addictions Studies Program at Governors State University in Illinois, and received his master's degree in social work from Loyola University. He is an international speaker in the behavioral science field whose presentations have reached thousands throughout the United States, Europe, Canada, and the Caribbean Islands. A partial list of clients includes Youth Outreach; Wisconsin Department of Corrections; the public school system in Nashville, Tennessee; Northwestern Hospital's Institute of Psychiatry; Hazelden Foundation; and United States Army, Navy, Air Force, and Marine Corps. Mark has spoken to these varied organizations on such subjects as mental health, diversity, stress management, empowering the homeless, clinical supervision, and treatment for adolescents, substance abuse, and criminal justice. The author of four books and numerous articles and manuals, Mark is also a contributor in two books in the Chicken Soup for the Soul series and has published twelve CDs on clinical strategies for working with adolescents. The recipient of the Barbara Bacon Award for outstanding contributions to the social work profession as a graduate of Loyola University of Chicago's School of Social Work, Mark is also the recipient of the Professional of the Year Award granted by the Illinois Addictions Counselor Certification Board for his work as a trainer and consultant. Learn more at www.onthemarkconsulting25.com.